roots&Branches

roots&Branches

CREATING INTERGENERATIONAL THEATER

ARTHUR STRIMLING

HEINEMANN
PORTSMOUTH, NH

Heinemann
A division of Reed Elsevier Inc.
361 Hanover Street
Portsmouth, NH 03801–3912
www.heinemanndrama.com

Offices and agents throughout the world

The author and publisher wish to thank those who have generously given permission to reprint borrowed material:

Poem from *Rumi: The Book of Love: Poems of Ecstasy and Longing* by Coleman Barks. Copyright © 2003 by Coleman Barks. Reprinted by permission of HarperCollins Publishers Inc.

Library of Congress Cataloging-in-Publication Data
Strimling, Arthur.
    Roots & branches : creating intergenerational theater / Arthur Strimling.
       p. cm.
    ISBN 0-325-00507-9
      1. Amateur theater. 2. Theater and the aged. I Title: Roots and branches.
II. Title.
PN3160.A34S77 2004
792.02'22—dc22   2003018524

Editor: Lisa A. Barnett
Production: Lynne Reed
Cover design: Jenny Jensen Greenleaf
Typesetter: Tom Allen
Manufacturing: Steve Bernier

Printed in the United States of America on acid-free paper
08 07 06 05 04 VP 1 2 3 4 5

To Barbara Myerhoff and Joseph Chaikin,
both of blessed memory.
You changed everything.

Contents

Acknowledgments

There is a kind of tree, the banyan, that produces immense forests, which appear from the ground to be comprised of countless individual trees. But in fact there is only one immense root under ground, and all those seemingly individual trees are part of one giant organism. And that is my image for this book: It is the product of what may seem to be many trees, but in fact they are all rooted together in the same soil. The leaves that are the pages of this book come from many wonderful minds and spirits, but all come from a common root that grows out from generation to generation.

First thanks to Linda Winston who first suggested that I turn a dozen years of Roots&Branches experience into a book. She and Anne Davis Basting were my sure guides through the unfamiliar terrain of book outlines and proposals.

Two collaborators have been at the heart of everything. In the early years, Christian McEwen was my partner in the workshops and scripting. She gave unstintingly of her gentle spirit, her deep literacy, and her great gift for charged intimate conversation. In recent years, David Schechter has been officially called Creative Consultant, which barely begins to describe his role in Roots&Branches. David shows us all over and over how to make the beautiful necessary and the necessary beautiful. I thank you both for your work and inspiration and for the pleasure of your company.

JASA, the Jewish Association for Services for the Aged (an agency of the UJA/Federation) was our home for thirteen years and we thank the Board and staff for their support. Special thanks to David Stern, Executive Director during most of our time at JASA, who actively promoted our work and our vision. David is a rare visionary in the social service world who understands the role of the arts in the changing landscape of aging. Professor Jan Cohen-Cruz of New York University's Tisch School of the Arts Theatre Program has been our link to most of the students who have worked with us. Jan is a powerful advocate for community-based theater, and Roots&Branches is only one of many companies that have reason to be grateful for her energy and passion. A.R.T./NY, thanks particularly to the good work of Ginny Louloudes, Jerry Homan, and Stephanie Bock, has provided a wonderful writing space and community of theater artists at 138 South Oxford Street.

Hugh Downs was for many years our honorary Chair, and lent his wisdom and prestige most generously. Now Barbara Barrie has taken over that role with great imagination, savvy, and energy. Both have been wonderful teachers. And thanks to all who have served so generously on our Council of Directors.

Anne Davis Basting, Peter and Susan Pitzele, Yvette Pollack, Lisa B. Segal, Trisha Arlin, Alicia Ostriker, Doug Stewart, and Eliza Roaring Springs read all or part of the manuscript at various stages and made invaluable suggestions. I am proud to have them as friends who can also be the best of colleagues. Their examples, encouragement, and love keep me going. Errors of taste, judgment and fact, however, are mine alone.

Lisa Barnett, my editor at Heinemann, has been unfailingly supportive and optimistic, as have the entire staff I dealt with there.

Many professionals have given generously and imaginatively to Roots&Branches. Thanks to them all, and particular acknowledgment to: Howard Pflanzer, who founded the JASA Theatre Ensemble and co-authored our early plays; Risa Jaroslow, Melinda Hunt, and Jason Kao Hwang for *Encounters at the Border*; set and costume designers Dawn Robyn Petrlik, Tine Kindermann, and Rosemary Ponzo; print designers Anita Marlene Merk and Lynn Fylak; composer/musicians Giancarlo Vulcano and the Steves: Steve Browman, Steve Elson, and Steve Weisberg; director Deborah Nitzberg; administrators Lauren Scott, Theda Zuckerman, and Ruth Weintraub; and production staff Patrick Lanczki, Tory Schaefer, Stephanie Blanton, and Bob Griffin. Working with you all has been an inspiration and a pleasure.

The Roots and Branches from which these leaves sprout have been my community for these dozen and more years. They have astonished me so often that it has become my normal state when I am with them.

Thursday afternoon has been the one time in the week that I can count on to lift my spirits and restore my belief in human nature and theater. Many more than this list have passed through, but these are the ones who were with us in both workshops and performance: Sabine Auf der Heyde, Mary Auyung, Dan Bacalzo, Bernie Basescu, Kaleo Bird, Matthew Boline, Jessica Burr, Laurence Checler, Cindy Chesler, Yim Chin, Rosa Cohen-Cruz, Joye Cook, Yvette DeBotton, Erica DeLaRosa, Anthony DiModica, David Dinolfo, Roz Dunn, Sol Frieder, Molly Gibeau, Millie Gold, Emily Goodridge, Juli Greenberg, Verna Hampton, Elizabeth Hargnett, Ariel Harmon, Ruth Hirsch, Esther Horne, Tenjin Ikeda, Jen Johnson, Robyn Katz, Minna Kolinsky, Samantha Lally, Dera Lee, Dawn Lerman, Nick Levy, Martha Libman, Zoe Lister-Jones, Michaela Lobel, Aaron Lorenz, Susannah Mackintosh, Emily Marks, Kelly Main, Sara Mayer, Annie McVey, Muriel Mervis, Sara Elizabeth Michaels, Michele Minnick, Frederick Mursch, Heather Norfleet, Bryan Peters, Yvette Pollack, Marcy Ried, Ofelia Rodriguez, Chazz Rose, Zachary Rothman-Hicks, Sam Schatsky, Lauren Scott, Ken Schneck, Molly Seif, Deena Selenow, Adele Shulim, Richard Sisk, Robert Sorrentino, Navah Steiner, Sara Stock-Mayo, Jessica Travis, Wei Du Ho, Selma Wernick, Al Wolf, Ian Young, and Lora Zuckerman.

Four Roots have left us; may their memories be for a blessing: Sam Isaacs, Etta Denbin, Ida Harnden and Clarence Carter.

In the banyan forest of my life, family is the core tree and always the source. Barney, Wolf, and two Sarahs rooted our family in America and passed on opportunity, good values, and family feeling. My mother, Edith Owen, showed me the challenges and pleasures of a life in the theater and continues to be a savvy, sassy source of wisdom and fun. By his words and example, my father, Arthur G. Steinberg, taught me the importance of vocation, or what Marge Piercy calls "work that is real." Jean Strimling teases the wind out of my pretensions as only a sister can. My branches, Eric and Ethan, who themselves have grown into magnificent trees, are my proudest creations. And the deepest thanks of all to *mi compañera* of valor, Lisa B. Segal, who magically manages to be both the solid trunk of our life together and the lithe, lovely bird on a branch, enchanting my life with her song.

Preface

This is a book about age. Not old age or middle age or teenage, but age. Age as a way of understanding, defining, and distinguishing us.

Age, like race or gender, is some mix of biology and history. Age is a definer. A stealth definer these days. These days age seems a strange perspective from which to understand the world. These days we are comfortable, if that's the word, with breaking things down along lines of race or ethnicity, religion, gender, or sexual preference. We are less comfortable with class as a definer, though we know it is there. But age? What is that? How can I define myself that way? There are seemingly no real distinctions to be made since age is something that happens to all of us (if we are lucky, as the sage wisecrack goes). I can never be black or brown, or Chinese. I would have to go to excruciating lengths to become a woman. While I could convert, everyone knows that at some level or other I can't ever stop being Jewish.

There was a brief time in my twenties, when age became terribly and absurdly relevant. The cry was, "Don't trust anyone over thirty!" Although no one with half a brain took it literally or even seriously, we also knew there was an undercurrent of truth there. And that was a recognition that we are defined by our times, that being over thirty could mean that you were so steeped in the 1950s, in Ike and the Cold War and organization man conformity and Pat Boone or Doris Day or formalist Modernism and what all else that you just couldn't free yourself for the revolution that was surely coming (unless of course you were Alan Ginsberg or Grace Paley or Dorothy Day or Chuck Berry, or for that matter, Fidel, Che, Mao, or Marx (Karl or Groucho)). It was as absurd, and as real, as all such broad classifications.

But this kind of thinking goes way back. One reason, the rabbis tell us, that the Hebrew people had to wander in the desert for forty years was so that the generation who had grown up as slaves in Egypt would all die out, and the promised land would not be sullied by their presence. The idea was that their *slaveness,* their history, was so deeply built into them that no amount of freedom could expunge it. In those days, it was "don't trust anyone over forty."

We name generations: the Lost Generation, the Civil Rights Generation, Boomers, Gen X, and so on. The labels imply something about the way that history has defined peoples' life experience, politics, or philosophy. And we all know how deeply different our outlooks can be from those of our parents and children. We know that some moments in history so sear us that our whole lives are affected—the Depression, WWII (which my parents call, simply, "The War," as if there were no others, and in a way, for them, there weren't), the Civil Rights Movement, Vietnam, the destruction of the World Trade Towers. These events affect our whole lives as deeply in their own way as those events we think of as *personal*—childhood, parenting, failure and success, loss, love, and death.

The word *aging* tends to be used in reference to *old* people, and that term can mean anything from sixty up, depending often on where you stand in the age range (gerontologists and others in the field now talk about *young old*, meaning sixties to about eighty, and *old old*). Aging, however, is in fact what we are doing all the time, all of our lives. We have that in common, as the poets are always trying to remind us.

And yet, the differences seem to matter more. Even to the poets. A dear friend, a poet of high repute, told me that after thirty years of loving teaching undergraduates, she can't stand it any more. They have no sense of history, she says. The Vietnam War might as well be the Trojan War. Their music and TV-based culture is alien. A dedicated progressive and feminist, she can't stand their *me first* morality, the product of growing up in the 1980s and 1990s.

And yet, again, we are all aging. All of us were young, and if we are young now, we expect to live to be the age of the others. And when that fact sinks in, really sinks in, true dialogue can begin. It takes between five and ten workshops in Roots&Branches. Then, for example, when the elder women (the *Roots* we call them) talked last season about the transforming influence of 1970s consciousness-raising groups on their lives, the young women (the *Branches*), who dissociate themselves from early feminism ("too strident," they say, "hysterical, separatist, unnecessary"), began to understand that these powerful elders they had come to look up to couldn't have become the tough, wise, salty, life-loving women they are without that radical break with their past. And the Roots women stopped resenting the young for their privileges and opportunities, and felt proud that they had done their generational job so well that this generation didn't have to go through it all again.

Through most of human history the generations, at least those who farmed or worked at crafts, were stuck together (for better or worse), interacting in known, set ways. The old taught the young what they needed to know to live the life that was inescapably prescribed for them. This made for a deeply traditional, conservative, and circumscribed world, one in which the individual existed only in reference to others. If you asked my aunt Annie, the last in my family who came from such a world, who she was, she would describe a network: whose daughter she was, whose sister, wife, aunt, cousin, and so on. She would also tell you that she was of a certain county where she lived her whole life and the town she had lived in for fifty years. That network was her self-description, and her pride lay in how she had served, honored, nursed, nurtured, and taught them. Aunt Annie was also a world traveler, an art collector, an avid reader, a great cook, a gardener, and a shrewd manager of her investments. She was proud of these accomplishments, but they were not who she was, they were in service to her true identity as she saw it. My mother on the other hand, born more than a decade later, is a classic American second-generation success story; she had a long and successful acting career and that's what she would tell you about if you asked. Of course she is proud of her children and grandchildren, but she is at least as proud to call herself an emancipated woman, defined by her individual accomplishments.

The world my aunt lived in was cohesive and whole in ways we can barely imagine. Now the individual's freedom is paramount, or supposed to be, and we seem always to be in pursuit of the next freedom. We cherish our freedom, our mobility, our individualism. But, if the cultural critics, politicians, religious leaders, and others are right, we miss something. Our individualism makes us feel (surprise!) alone, cut off from community, family ties, even friendship. So how can we, without giving up any of the freedom and mobility we cherish, recover some of the connectedness we miss? Roots&Branches is many things—a theater group, a community, a teaching and learning center, a continuing experiment, a service provider. But at heart Roots& Branches is a response to that question, and so is this book.

Figure I–1. Samantha Lally and Molly Seif in *An Appalling Old Lady*, set by
Tine Kindermann. Photograph by Elena Olivo.

Introduction

A Snapshot of Roots & Branches

Imagine yourself in a large hall watching a performance of *Romeo and Juliet*. Your fellow audience members, several hundred of them, are elderly, which means they are mostly women. They have come in groups, on busses from senior centers around the city. They are attentive and enjoying the show, but they are not a decorous audience. The rustle of candy wrappers and plastic bags never ceases. A woman with big platinum hair says something in a loud stage whisper to her friend. But it isn't loud enough; "What?" says friend, turning up her hearing aid. Several sharp shooshes echo from around the hall, but Big Hair is undaunted and repeats in a voice that no longer even pretends to whisper: "That one is so pretty, but why is she wearing a ring in her nose?" "Terrible," says her friend. More shooshing. More comments—on the story or the actors' looks or costumes; more shooshing. And so it goes. But then comes a line they all know—"Romeo, Romeo, wherefore art thou Romeo?" or "Good night, good night, a thousand times goodnight"—and suddenly the whole audience is swaying to the rhythm of the moment and speaking along with our eighty-five-year-old Juliet.

Because this is no traditional *Romeo and Juliet*. First of all, the actors are either college age—eighteen to twenty-two—or elderly—sixty-five to eighty-six. And the setting has been moved from Renaissance Verona, to a modern Love Boat-type ship, the SS *Verona*, on her Shakespearean cruise. Three star-crossed couples of different ages, and age mixes, have met and fallen passionately in love on this cruise.

It has come to Juliet's death scene. Instead of the crypt, we are on the deck of the ship. Midnight; a cardboard moon hangs overhead.

1

Our octogenarian Juliet, played by Molly, creeps out to meet her unlikely Romeo, handsome dashing twenty-two-year-old Matt. He is mad with love, smitten by her wisdom, clarity, and fiery lust for life. He wants to run off with her and travel the world; even proposes marriage, to which Molly cries, "No, never again!" Devastated, Matt threatens to jump overboard if she will not go with him. He hangs over the ship's rail and cries,

> Eyes, look your last. Death,
> Thou desperate pilot, now at once run on
> The dashing rocks thy seasick weary bark

The elderly women in the audience are loving this; they have more than willingly suspended their disbelief. One yells, "I'll take him if she won't!"

Suddenly, Molly grabs her chest and slumps. Matt runs to her, enfolds her in his arms and calls for help. All the other actors rush on stage and gather around. Molly/Juliet, fading, blesses her young love and, with a final, "Good night, good night, parting is such sweet sorrow, that I shall say good night till it be. . . . ," she dies. There is an agonized silence.

The audience stirs. Big Hair "whispers" loudly into her deaf friend's ear, "Is she acting or is she really sick?" "Or dead," says friend loud enough for everyone to hear. From another row: "Call a doctor!" Across the room: "Shoosh, it's part of the play." The suspense is becoming unbearable.

This is exactly the moment the cast, writer, and director had worried about several months before when we first imagined this scene. We knew that if you are doing *Romeo and Juliet*, even a very deconstructed version, there has to be a death scene. But death is not an easy subject for the elderly. They are surrounded by it, like soldiers in war. And, like soldiers, they face death with stoic courage. But they don't like to talk about it.

So we worried: how to handle this delicate subject? Our dramaturg, Christian McEwan, and I decided that if we could construct a scene that worked for the older members of the company, it would probably be okay for our elder audiences. So, we began by asking Molly and Matt to improvise the death scene—just the two of them, without the rest of the company watching. Molly, born for melodrama, a diva to her DNA, improvised a twenty-minute dying valedictory, more aria than speech. We tape-recorded everything, transcribed it, and then, whittled it into a draft of a scene.

At the next workshop, Molly and Matt read the scene for the whole cast, playing it to the hilt. When it was over, there was a silence, and then all hell broke loose. The young actors, college acting students from NYU, loved the scene, found it moving, funny, and true to the original play. But the elders hated it. "Death? Death is not a nice afternoon's entertainment." "I have a heart condition, I don't want to think about it." "We'll upset our audiences." And so on. The argument went on and on.

Now, this is the only time in twelve years that I can remember our intergenerational ensemble breaking down completely along generational lines, so this was hardly a typical situation. But here it was: young idealistic artists fighting for truth and beauty, versus folks who don't need a play to teach them about the sting of death. The workshop ended at an impasse. What to do?

Flash forward to the performance. Molly lies inert in Matt's arms. The other actors are gathered around them; the audience is getting restive. Suddenly, from the upper deck of the SS *Verona*, Muriel pipes up:

MURIEL: Wait a minute, we can't have a death in this play.

IDA: Right. We seniors have to cope with this situation every day of our lives. Death is not a pleasant afternoon's entertainment.

SAM: We need a happy ending. I have a heart condition. Death depresses me.

KELLY: But this is *Romeo and Juliet*. In *Romeo and Juliet* the lovers die. It's what's supposed to happen. It's the tragedy of fate.

MINNA: Romeo and Juliet are young people, like you. When young people die the audience knows it's only a play. But when it's older people, then they think it's true.

CHAZZ: I don't agree that we should try to protect the audience. For me, bringing up death is a positive thing. That's what art is for— to bring up the issues that are too painful.

MINNA: Why doesn't she just have a few pains in her chest? Then she could say, "You almost gave me a heart attack!"

IAN: That would be censorship! Your version is just painting a smiley face on the truth.

KELLY: Right. A play isn't supposed to be just entertainment.

ETTA: Enough tears in life!

AL: Eat, drink and be merry, that's my philosophy!

The whole argument from the workshop months before is reenacted on stage over the "dead" body of Juliet. By now all but the dimmest in the audience understand that this is a stage death, and they listen interestedly to the dialogue. There are murmurs of agreement, mostly with the elders, some with the side of truth and artistic integrity. And just as the argument is coming to a head, Molly pops up and announces fiercely:

MOLLY: But this is my death scene, and I love it! I'm eighty-five years old and I never got to play Juliet until now. And anyway, everybody knows Juliet dies in the end."

And with that she plops back down into Matt's arms as the audience howls and applauds.

Welcome to Roots&Branches Theater.

That moment crystallized everything we are about:

- Young and old working together, successfully, pleasurably, and intimately.
- Differences and similarities between young and old acknowledged, played with, and celebrated.
- Stereotypes, assumptions, hopes, and clichés about age are examined and challenged, revealing their falsehood . . . and truth.
- A collaborative process is reflected and quoted in the play.
- And a good time had by all.

From Generation to Generation

But why intergenerational theater? Is there a real need for it, a vision behind this, or is it simply a nice way to pass time for some young and old people and their audiences? That would be justification enough, but this book is going to argue that much more is going on, that we have lost an essential part of ourselves that can only be regained through lasting, intimate contact between the generations.

Age Segregation

Alice, now living in a beachfront community on Long Island, remembers her childhood on a farm in Minnesota more than eighty years ago. "We were ten children. I was the oldest, and now I'm the only one left. We were so many because they needed the hands. We were free labor. The boys worked the fields with Father. Grandpa walked around and gave them hell if they were lazy or did something stupid. I took care of the little ones, so it was natural that I became a teacher. And my sisters cleaned house and helped with the laundry, which was terrible hard work. And every day, while Mother cooked breakfast and nursed babies, Grandma would sit us girls down and dole out the day's chores."

I'm leading a workshop in a junior high school in a suburb of Minneapolis. The school is near a retirement home, and the plan is for the students to interview the seniors about life in Minneapolis in the "old days." I am here to help the kids design their interviews. I tell them, "Food is a good subject. People love to talk about food—recipes, holiday meals, and everyday meals; what they ate when they were kids like you. And even things like what table manners they were taught and who sat where at the table at family meals." I'm warming to my subject, but after a few minutes I realize I have lost my audience. This line of subject matter is drawing complete blanks. Suddenly it dawns on me; I ask, "How many of you eat one meal a day with the whole family sitting down together at the dining room table?" Not one hand goes up. "Once a week?" Two or three hands go up—Friday night dinner or Sunday after church. But at least twenty-five out of the thirty kids in the class have no idea what I am talking about. They don't eat meals, they "graze." "When I'm hungry I just nuke something or order a pizza." They eat alone or with siblings or friends, in front of the TV. Their parents rush out in the morning and come home too late in the evening for there to be any hope of a family meal. And weekends are just as busy, or Mom and Dad are simply too exhausted.

These two stories reflect a reality of our rapidly modernizing society. In a couple of generations family life has changed faster and more than in all previous human history. And most of us did not choose it. Change became the medium for American life. Progress, innovation, adaptation are watchwords; continuity, tradition, and such language are mostly used for sentimental spin.

For most of human history families lived together in the same place, following the same trade or farming the same land from generation to generation. When children became adults, they did what had been done forever as far as they knew; the same work, cooked the same meals, sang the same songs, prayed to the same God, and told their children the same stories, probably in the same words, that they had heard themselves.

Obviously there are great disadvantages to such a world: innovation, entrepreneurship, individuality, change itself are sacrificed to tradition and continuity. The pressure to conform is total—think of *The Scarlet Letter* or *Fiddler on the Roof*. My grandfather, like many other immigrants, left the old world and came to America to escape such stifling limitations, and he made himself into a man his father could barely recognize.

Like my grandfather, we gain a lot from all this change: mobility, personal freedom, escape from hidebound traditions, a much higher standard of living. And the list could go on. But we also lose some things, and maybe some baby is being thrown out with the bathwater of tradition.

Take mobility for example. My wife and I live in New York, my parents in Ohio, my sister in Toronto, one son and my granddaughter in San Francisco, and the other son in Portland, Maine. We all love where we live and are grateful for the mobile society that makes it possible. We keep in touch by phone and email and visit once or twice a year. We are a close-knit family, but we are not close by. If there is a crisis or a celebration, we gather, but if someone has a cold and needs a box of Kleenex, we don't call each other, in fact most wouldn't know about the cold at all. Our day-to-day lives are lived with other people, people from other places and backgrounds, who have no tie to us that comes close to blood, and who often disappear to be replaced by new friends, neighbors, or co-workers.

Mobility has gained us a lot, but it has also cost us. As Alice's story at the beginning of this section suggests, in more traditional cultures each generation has significant roles to play, everyone is needed. Elders possess skills and knowledge of weather and markets honed over decades, which they pass on to their children, who pass it on to theirs, so the choices anyone makes are informed not only by their own experience and wisdom, but that of generations.

Today, however, the skills our grandparents practiced in their work lives are as obsolete as the buggy whip or a mustard plaster. And in our practical culture that obsolescence becomes generalized into a sense that the old themselves are obsolete and can be shuffled aside into *retirement* (a very new concept in human history).

But there are kinds of life experience that do not become obsolete. The wisdom of a life well lived does not change—all of us are children and adolescents; go to school, work, learn about sex, friendship and love, money and family, success and failure, loyalty and betrayal, loneliness, self-mastery, about how to accept aging and death. This kind of knowledge, as the Bible and great literature teach us, does not change from generation to generation, and can be transmitted. If the generations are in touch enough for it to happen. But if your family is like mine and most in America, the grandparents live hundreds, even thousands of miles away from grandchildren, and what they can transmit is mostly limited to love and presents. These are certainly important, but Roots&Branches and this book are based on the premise that a lot is missing.

Now no one can turn the clock around and return to past ways. I for one certainly don't want to. So, if old and young are to have more than superficial contact we must reinvent the generation-to-generation wheel.

The first thing to recognize is that while we may not be near our own grandparents or grandchildren, there are lots of people of different generations living nearby. But in the normal course of our lives we don't have much contact. Those young people may be hanging around the mall where you shop, or those old people might be taking up the benches in the park, but we barely notice. What's needed, as part of the solution, are programs that bring generations together in constructive enjoyable ways, that allow them to remain in contact long enough to know and appreciate each other, that allow for that mysterious transmission of love and understanding that happens below the radar of the outer activities.

7

The Uses of Reminiscence

Excerpt: Two Selections from *Playing Lear*

The first selection is a rant delivered at top volume during the storm scene. In workshop, the actors had improvised their own rants inspired by quotes from Lear's "Blow winds, and crack your cheeks." The scene weaves between Lear and these rants:

LEAR: Blow winds, and crack your cheeks! Rage! Blow!
　　You cataracts and hurricanes, spout
　　Till you have drenched the steeples, drowned the cocks!
　　. . . Here I stand your slave,
　　A poor, infirm, weak and despised old man.
YVETTE: (*Shaking her fists at the heavens*) You never accepted me,
　　Mother! You never even knew me! I know a lot of kids think
　　they're adopted, but I had to be. 'A poor, infirm, weak old'
　　woman? Hah! More like a stupid, uneducated, cold woman!

Later, after the recognition and reconciliation between Lear and Cordelia, there is a sequence of (more or less) *reconciliation* moments. Between the actors and the demons they struggle with in their own stories. This is Yvette's:

YVETTE: (*Calling as she moves DR*) Muriel, come be my dead mama. I
　　didn't make peace with you before you died.
MURIEL: (*Stands DL, arms folded, grim expression*) No you didn't.
YVETTE: Maybe it's not too late now.
MURIEL: I think it's too late. I'm dead already thirty years.
YVETTE: (*Pleading*) Come back and listen.
MURIEL: Can I?
YVETTE: Yeah. I will you back.
MURIEL: (*Tone of "Don't do me any favors"*) Thank you.
YVETTE: And I will send you away again when I'm through with you.
MURIEL: That's you!
YVETTE: Y'know, I always thought of you as a timid, frightened
　　woman who passed on all her fears to me.
MURIEL: Insults? For this you brought me back. More insults?
YVETTE: May I finish?

MURIEL: (*Grudging*) Go ahead.

YVETTE: But then I had to make a speech at my grandson's bar mitzvah, telling him what legacy I was bringing from my past, and I found myself talking about you. About how at the age of sixteen you left a little shtetl in Poland. And came to America, and made a life for yourself. It took a lot of courage, and I never acknowledged that.

MURIEL: (*Angrily*) Growing up in Poland and coming here so young, it does bad things to the soul, I mean very bad things. And you know, your father and I, we never had any fun, no good times. All those years in that damn grocery store, day in, day out. But I did the best I could.

YVETTE: I know. And now that you're gone all these years, I can see the good things in you. The things I never saw when you were alive. And all I can say is, I'm sorry.

MURIEL: (*Long pause, then more angrily*) It's about time!

YVETTE: (*Pause*) Well, we made a start didn't we?

MURIEL: (*Turning to exit*) Yeah, I guess.

YVETTE: Will you come back again whenever I need you to?

MURIEL: (*Over her shoulder*) Sure—if I'm not busy minding the store . . . ![1]

One day in the late 1950s, I was in high school, a social worker took me aside and told me to stop encouraging my grandmother to reminisce. "Reminiscence," she said, "is the high road to senility." I knew instinctively that she was wrong. It was simply too much fun for both of us, her telling and me listening. So after that, when she told me stories, Grandma and I closed the door. I thought I was just keeping her company; it wasn't until years later that I and the field of gerontology realized how much else was going on.

Reminiscence, telling stories about your life, is associated with old age, but it is an essential tool throughout life. A child comes in weeping and seeks your sympathy with a story that blames the booboo on the sibling. Later, in the dating years, "Tell me the story of your life," is a standard come-on, and you tell the intriguing version or the boring version, depending on how interested you are. In midlife the past is your resume, your ticket to opportunity. And always reminiscence is a way to connect.

In old age, however, the stakes rise drastically. Now most of life is memory; now the end is approaching; now remembering becomes a central task.

The psychiatrist, Robert Butler, in an essay called "The Life Review," and the anthropologist Barbara Myerhoff, whose great book *Number Our Days* and her Academy Award-winning film of the same name, have inspired two generations of anthropologists, social workers, gerontologists, artists, and many others to do exactly the opposite of what that social worker told me.[2] We now understand that reminiscence is a major developmental task for the elderly, essential in the process of aging well and dying well. Broadly, the uses of reminiscence in old age include:

- *Projecting Oneself into the Future*. Telling stories to those who will remain after you, in the hope, not only that they will remember you, but also as you hope to be remembered.
- *Passing the Torch*. Again, telling younger generations stories that you hope will infuse them with some wisdom, truth, or belief, or fire them to pursue some cause you believe is important to the future.
- *Life Review*. This is Butler's title for the personal use of memory, in which the ultimate audience is the self. Broadly, the developmental goal is to see your life as an integrated and meaningful whole; to come to terms with your life as part of coming to terms with dying. The process often involves returning over and over to unresolved and painful events or relationships in search of an interpretation, a telling, that resolves or mediates the struggle and integrates it into a nourishing sense of self.

Anyone who works with the elderly sees and, these days, probably encourages these processes constantly. Often in real life, they are halting, circular, slow, and somewhat opaque, but in theater we can compress and intensify. Although the two earlier pieces of script are almost word for word as they came out in workshop, they probably represent only a small part of a process that has gone on for decades. Still, Yvette's rant and later attempt at reconciliation with her long dead mother are a rich and complex weave of the uses of reminiscence. And they demonstrate both the importance of reminiscence to the work of Roots&Branches and the value of art to successful reminiscence.

First it is important to note that Yvette is not a troubled or unhappy person. In fact, she is a prime example of successful aging; accomplished, vital, wise, and enviably blessed with an international circle of friends and devoted children and grandchildren. And yet, here she is in her late seventies still struggling with her long dead mother, still telling the story, still trying to "work it out." Don't we ever get over our parents?

Well, no, as our experience in Roots&Branches proves over and over again. So what is going on? How is she *using* reminiscence and how does performance come into the process?

At the plot level, we first see a woman raging at her mother. She could be speaking from almost any age. It is a rage planted in childhood, still burning, still justified in her eyes. The woman in the reconciliation scene is speaking in the present or very recent past. The rage is still there, but it is balanced, not diluted, by an understanding that has come with time. There is a Jewish tradition that angels are different from humans because angels, in their purity, can carry only one feeling at a time, whereas humans are complex; we simultaneously carry many feelings, even contradictory ones, within ourselves. One kind of wisdom is accepting that complexity, and that is what we see happening here; Yvette is still angry at her mother, but she accepts that there are also "good things" about her.

Repetition, the revisiting of events and relationships, is an essential element of life review, and this is where Roots&Branches plays an interesting role. In dozens of rehearsals and about thirty performances over two years, Yvette lived these feelings and stories over and over, giving herself the opportunity to go deeper and deeper into them. The words do not change, but her relationship to them does: "This is the first time I had any compassion for my mother. Performing this scene over and over made me more objective toward her. At first I would come off stage crying after I performed it, but eventually I became more objective and I could talk about her without becoming hysterical and emotional."

As she tells about honoring her mother's life at her grandson's bar mitzvah, Yvette conveys messages within messages within messages. First she establishes her credentials: "I had to make a speech at my grandson's bar mitzvah." That is, "I am the grandmother of a boy who has successfully completed a major rite of passage, and what's more I am a significant figure in this family because I was asked to speak." Certainly it is essential to any of the tasks of successful aging that one sees oneself and is seen by others as worthy of being remembered. But there is much more going on.

We hear Yvette struggling within herself to acknowledge that this "stupid, uneducated, cold woman" who "never accepted me" is also someone who, by overcoming terrible adversity and suffering, paved the way for her to make it into the American mainstream so her children and grandchildren could climb even higher. This progression from raging anger in the storm scene toward a more complex and balanced understanding is classic life review: retelling a painful story, choosing different facts from the infinity available to create for oneself a version that feels truthful, whole, and perhaps even nourishing. This happens, of course, only in the scene; at the actual bar mitzvah, none of the conflict was revealed. Other agendas were operating there.

A bar mitzvah is the ritual passing of the torch of Jewish identity from generation to generation, assuring the continuance of the Jewish people. In asking her to speak, the family acknowledges that continuity, and Yvette takes it back beyond memory for the bar mitzvah boy. By seeking to plant his great-grandmother's memory firmly in her grandson, Yvette saves her for one more generation from disappearing into the mists of time; she has, in Barbara Myerhoff's ringing phrase, "erased oblivion." The message we hear is, "Even this woman whom I can never forgive, even she must be remembered." And the message behind the message is, "Don't forget me! Don't forget me! Just as I plant an indelible memory of my mother in you, so you must find the means to plant me firmly in the future."

But even having accomplished so much at the bar mitzvah, Yvette's urgency to use the past is not satisfied. She brings it first to Roots&Branches and then the play, performing this part of her life for thousands of people. The sight of her ranting against her long dead mother, her fist stabbed into the air, was stunning. And her performance with Muriel of the reconciliation scene was simultaneously searing and hilarious. In terms of projecting herself into the future, Yvette carries her story far beyond the usual parameters of reminiscence. My grandmother told her stories to me and perhaps one or two others, but Yvette literally *told* thousands. In sheer Darwinian terms, she has vastly increased her chances of being remembered.

Kinds of Senior Theater

There are hundreds of senior theater groups across the United States, in Canada, Europe, Australia, and Japan. China, too, is inaugurating senior theater. Practitioners of creative dramatics, people's theater, and avant-garde experimental groups of the 1960s and 1970s adapted their methods for working with older adults. Now, senior groups spring up at senior centers, senior residences, professional theater troupes, as well as established community theaters. Professor Anne Davis Basting defines four basic agendas:

- Groups who are mainly meeting to read or stage plays for recreation. They may or may not perform, but the goal is their own enjoyment.
- Groups that primarily want to serve their community. These groups perform in nursing homes, hospitals, or for groups of troubled children. Even in prisons, as Encore Theatre of Eugene, Oregon does. They share their memories and stories with those who might benefit from their energy and wisdom, and sometimes mentor the young people in doing theater of their own.
- Groups whose main interests are artistic. Some are highly professional. Their actors either were professionals or they have become professional late in life. They are in it for the challenge of being artists.
- Groups that want to use their performances to make social and political change. They take on the healthcare industries and government policies through agitprop performances.[3]

Professor Basting found that most groups pick one or two of these elements and focus on them. Groups formed for recreational purposes might also share performances with nursing homes. But Professor Basting found that Roots&Branches is unique among senior troupes, because it takes on all four of these aims. We are certainly recreational—pleasure is at the heart of any art, and our workshops are central weekly events in the lives of almost everyone who participates.

13

We serve audiences, elderly and young, who don't traditionally get to see theater. Our artistic goals are both a motivation in themselves, and we believe that our plays must be produced and performed at the highest possible artistic levels if we are to serve the social goals of celebrating the beauty, wisdom, and power of the elderly and build bonds between old and young.

Who Should Read This Book?

This is a book with a couple of missions as well as practical purposes. On the broadest level this is a meditation on age as an unnoticed and unattended aspect of our multicultural society and therefore of interest to anyone who aging; that is, anyone. As an extension of that, I hope that readers will be inspired to engage with these issues, to initiate or participate in intergenerational arts work. This is also a book about making theater that can be read and used in different ways and for different reasons.

Intergenerational Theater and Other Arts

If you are a student or professional in theater, social or group work, drama therapy, or simply interested in intergenerational arts, this book can be used as a manual, a how-to textbook. In the detailed portrait of how Roots&Branches theater works, you will find what you need to go out and do it yourself.

Community-based art like this is not directly translatable from one setting to another. In artspeak it is "site specific." Each site offers unique problems and opportunities, and your task will be to take what you learn in this book and translate it into a program that will work where you are. Perhaps the younger contingent aren't college students but high school age. That would make for very different tones and sets of issues for the group to engage. If you are a senior center director or school administrator eager to start a program, maybe you can't find a theater teacher/director, but there is a terrific dancer or visual artist ready to go. Give them this book. It will help them to plan their program, get it up and running, and make the right moves along the way.

Ensemble Theater Making

Roots&Branches creates plays through an ensemble process that has its roots in the Open Theatre, Peter Brooke's International Centre for Theatre Research (CIRT), the Talking Band, the Wooster Group, and others, a movement that started in the late 1960s, and became prominent in the 1970s and early 1980s. Their approaches and methods have been adapted and evolved by Roots&Branches and many other directors and groups. But the basic premise remains: The actors in the ensemble work with the director and writers, musicians, designers, and others over a period of months or even years to create completely original work.

If you are a student of acting, directing, dramaturgy, playwriting, or other theater-related arts, you will find here a detailed description not only of how one ensemble process works, but also the inner dynamics and strategies of an ensemble. It is a powerful way of making theater, with its own particular difficulties and opportunities, and they will all be gone into in some depth in this book.

Community-Based Theater

In the late 1960s and 1970s, when the Ensemble movement emerged and flowered, there was a politics of community underlying these theatrical visions and styles. To some extent that politics continues in the Community-Based Theater movement today. Groups like Cornerstone Theatre, the Negro Ensemble, the Women's Project, The 52nd Street Project, Theatre for the Blind, and the many nationality-based groups across the country are motivated not only by a theatrical vision, but also by the desire to use their theater to nourish some underserved community, be it poor people, people of color, women, the blind, or in our case a vision of a world less segregated by age.

Roots&Branches is a community-based theater that tries to build community at several levels: the company itself, the elderly and those in the many professions who serve them, young people, and the larger society as a whole.

Finally, I hope anyone who reads this, at any age, will enjoy it as an account of an experiment in building a small world of creativity and friendship; as a love story.

How to Use This Book

This is not a cookbook. You will find relatively few paradigms, lists of warm-up exercises, improvisations, or questions for discussion. All of these can be found in profusion in other books. Over the years we have adapted dozens of exercises to the needs of a particular subject or moment. Any warm up, improvisation or other method can be adapted to this work.

Where I do describe techniques in detail, however, I suggest that you try them yourself and see what happens. Compare your results with ours. If the exercise works for you, great. If not, discard it. It's like trying on a sweater: You don't really know how it will look or feel until you put it on, look in the mirror, and dance around in it. Then, if it's right, buy it; if not put it back on the rack.

So start with techniques that are familiar and comfortable, and adapt. For example, if you like to roll down and up your spine as part of a warm up, teach it. But, you have to realize that elderly bodies that haven't exercised much will have limited range. So you need to make it clear that however far they can go is fine, and they shouldn't push themselves. Also, invite those who are still nervous to try it sitting down. At this level, it's all basically common sense and sensitivity.

I will also emphasize over and over that every situation and group is unique. That means that you can't take anything here and expect to be able to use it exactly as it is presented. The key word is *adapt*. Once you understand what we do, and have a good sense of how it works in our context, look at your own context and imagine how to adapt to your situation, your vision, your actors, and your community. Or even better, allow what is described here to inspire you to invent something altogether new.

That is the goal: to inspire you. If I am able to communicate even a fraction of the pleasure, creativity, challenge, learning, wisdom, and sheer fun of the past twelve years with Roots&Branches, then I think it will inspire you to go out and try to create something of your own.

1

A Chapter Called "Me"

Excerpt from *Growing Up/Growing Down*[4]

(*To create* Growing Up/ Growing Down (A Fairy Tale or Two), *we explored the fairy tales we remembered from childhood or from telling our children and grandchildren. We realized that inside each of us there lives a princess, a prince, a fairy queen, enchanted frogs, wolves, ogres, an ugly duckling and . . . an aged crone. The elder women were outraged by the bad rap old women get in fairy tales, so they set out to create a new paradigm.*

At several stages in the play, Muriel has appeared as Betty Fairy Godmother Freidan, bringing her wisdom to counter Beautiful Princess/Barbie Doll/Marry and Live Happily Ever After iconography so common in fairy tales, ancient and modern. Each time she appears she passes out flyers advertising a lecture. Finally, the whole cast gather around her (including Bernie, the one man in this show), and applaud her entrance enthusiastically.)

MURIEL: Greetings! And welcome to "Afternoons in the Womb Room." As most of you probably know, I'm Betty Fairy Godmother Freidan. Thank you for coming today to my lecture/demonstration on "The Three Stages of Womanhood."

The first stage is "The Maiden" or "Princess."
The second is "The Mother" or "Queen."
The third, and most advanced stage is "The Crone" or "Witch."

Now, The Crone is often described in fairy tales as a figure who is bitter, withered and dry. But doesn't that strike you as just a teensy weensy bit sexist?

I would like to take this opportunity to apply quite a different adjective to this stage of life: "Juicy!"

Hit it, girls! (*Music comes up. Betty and other Roots sing*)

> They tell ya that wine gets better with age
> Well, honey, I have reached the vinegar stage
> Which is to say I'm tasty and tart
> I do what I feel like doin, straight from the heart
>
> Sure, once I was young and girlish like you
> I batted my eyes and sighed and blushed a bit too
> But Gloria Stei-nem finished all that
> Instead of a Barbie doll, desiring a whole new do
> She got me to throw my bra on the barbie-q
>
> And now I live happily on my own
> This princess has thrown away her throne
> The seeds of sedition have been sown,
> Just call me a bold bitch, good witch, juicy crone!
>
> They tell ya that life is full of hard knocks
> Well . . . honey, I've turned in my stockings for socks
> Tho glamour is swell, hell, candor is gold
> And, I'm growing grey and greater as I grow old
> Sure men have a taste for sugar and spice,
> But when a crone walks by,
> They never look twice.
>
> But if a real meal is what you crave
> instead of a yogurt shake
> rip into a juicy steak
> come watch what the kitchen witch
> CAN BITCHIN MAKE!

MURIEL: "Recipe for a Juicy Crone!"
In a sturdy well worn pot put:

(*Each part of the recipe is spoken by a Root, who mimes throwing it into a pot held by Branches, who "scat" under.*)

A pinch of libidinous youth
1/8 of a cup of real paprika from the Old Country
A splash of grey curls, iridescent
3 cups of Dewars, straight up
A liberal sprinkling of liver spots
1 pint tobacco juice (already spat)
2 tufts of nose hair
A dash of chili pepper
Two glistening fox eyes
Two lascivious licorice lips
a smidgeon of good ole lefty politics (*All Sing "Solidarity Forever . . ."*)
Oodles of moonlight

Allow ingredients to simmer on a low flame for at least sixty-five years, stirring occasionally.
Now, pour the mixture onto one VERY Human Being, preferably choice or prime. (*A bright cloth "pours" out of the pot onto a Branch, covering her completely. Roots gather around her and mime actions as they hide her from the audience*)

Rub vigorously, until mostly absorbed.
Just before serving, mix together equal parts Experience and Age.
Season with Education to taste.
Pour on a liberal amount of really good quality Lovin'.
And marinate until tender and wise
And for best results,

ALL: Serve warm.

Instead of half-baked, now I'm full-blown
Instead of a wisp, I'm flesh and bone
This tree has a trunk that's fully grown
A beautiful bold bitch,
Good witch,
Juicy crone!
I may not have flaxen hair,

But babe I got balls to spare!
Beware as I blare my baritone!

This mama's a joooooooo-uicy crone!!
A juicy crone! Yeah!
(*The cloth pops off revealing that the young woman has been magically replaced by ninety-seven-year-old Molly, who hits a "here I am" pose*)[5]

Beginnings

A bright, energetic young woman sits in my office picking my brain about how to start an intergenerational theater group in her home town. "I'm not really qualified," she says. "You're right," I say, "But go ahead anyway." It's safe to say that no one is really qualified—well maybe Tyrone Guthrie—but like most of us, this young woman has far more passion and vision than knowledge and experience.

She still demurs, wanting some formula, so then I tell her something like, "If you have the desire, you will figure out how to do it; you will bring people together; you will find space, money (barely enough, but enough), volunteers, tech support; and you will find audiences. Your situation will be unique in many ways, so the precedents, including ours, are only partly useful. And, if you are anything like me, you will make a lot of mistakes, and you will learn from them and go on. Samuel Beckett, as always, puts it pithily: 'Fail again. Try again. Fail better.'"

About twenty years ago, I was asked to train a group of at-risk youth to record the life stories of elders at an assisted living facility in the far northern end of Manhattan. I was a working actor then, and I had been making some plays out of the life stories I had heard at the senior center. I knew nothing about at-risk youth, and I had no idea how to proceed, but ignorance is a great courage-maker, so I said sure.

Most of the elders living in the residence were German Jews, who had lived in this neighborhood for forty or fifty years. Older than the century, they came from solid middle-class families in "civilized" pre-WWI Germany. They had lived through the Great War, some winning commissions and medals, and established themselves as "good" Germans.

And then their world was torn from them. Some escaped, some went into hiding, some were driven into the lowest rungs of hell. But they survived, often barely alive and with nothing but the prisoner uniforms on their backs, which made them the lucky ones, especially because they were in America. And here, in a remote corner of Manhattan, North of Harlem, far from the bright lights of midtown, they forged an enclave and started over; made homes, businesses, and families.

And they prospered. Their rigorous educations and culture served them well in postwar America. Now, in retirement, they could afford a comfortable, very well-run residence, where they lived independently in their own apartments. They were proud, cultured in the old-world way, and refined. Their children had climbed high on the greasy pole of the American dream. Over and over they would boast that Henry Kissinger was a graduate of the high school right across the street. But the cost of their children's success was that they lived far away, visited rarely, and viewed their parents as exotic burdensome anachronisms.

So their enclave had narrowed to themselves. Many of their generation had died, others had moved to Florida or Arizona. The neighborhood changed. New waves of immigrants from Central America swept in. The old delicatessen was now a Bodega, stocking platanos, guavas, dried cod, and even goat meat, but a good brisket or strudel was nowhere to be found. The kids now attending the high school they bragged about hung out and played Salsa music loud, dressed "immodestly," and proudly spoke Spanish or the hybrid called Span-glish. They struck these decorous elders as disrespectful, rude, ignorant, and threatening. The crime rate had risen; some residents had been mugged; many were afraid to go out; and the neighborhood was plagued by drug dealers. They felt under siege in their own homes. It was as if the world had moved right out from them. They hadn't gone anywhere, but still they were living in a new country. And this new country was far less welcoming than their first America had been. In a wonderful multicultural twist, they called themselves the last of the Mohicans.

The young people I was to train and supervise were from this new world. They were eighteen-year-olds who had dropped out of school and been in trouble with the law. A new program called The City Volunteer Corps offered them jobs, medical insurance, education, and money toward college if they got their high school diplomas and stuck it out in the Corps for a year. The volunteer part meant that they had to work at this residence, and, from their viewpoint, they had been turned into servants, doing the menial things that people of color do for white people—cleaning, wheeling them around, shopping, and so on.

For four days a week, Friday was turned over to my "Life Stories" project. I was supposed to get these frightened old people to open up, one on one, to these angry kids, who were supposed to become informed, attentive interviewers. Right!

When I arrived for my first day, things were not going well. In the morning I met with the kids. They had their street faces on; most just slumped sullenly in their chairs, picking at the muffins I had brought. The few who would talk let me know that the people in this place were stuck up racists who ordered them around. And even worse, they were old and ugly and couldn't talk right. The Life Stories project inspired only deeper slumping and deader eyes. Until I pulled out tape recorders and had them interview each other. The machines turned them on—some started rapping into them—and talking to each other transformed the room. With me out of the picture, they became animated, sophisticated in their own ways, cordial, caring, even loving in the boisterous, libidinous ways of youth. I began to understand that their sullenness toward me had more to do with shyness and lack of training in the social graces than actual hostility.

And I realized that these kids, semiliterate at best, knew nothing of the world these old people came from, and cared less. They had heard of World War II and Hitler, for example, but they did not know that the two had anything to do with each other. If they thought about it, they figured that if there was a WWII there must have been a World War I, but that's as far as it went. They had heard of concentration camps and were interested because it related to slavery, which they took personally. But they had no idea that the Holocaust had anything to do with WWII or Hitler or when it might have happened. When I told them that some of the old people they would interview had been in concentration camps, they began to get interested.

After lunch it was the old peoples' turn, and in their own ways, they were as difficult as the kids had been in the morning. "How could I tell these hoodlums anything?" they protested. "They have no manners, they're ignorant, they dress slovenly, they're just waiting for a chance to rob us." "I would never let them in my apartment, much less tell them about my life," and so on.

It didn't look good until I suggested that this could be an opportunity to teach, to show these kids that history is real lived experience, not just stuff in textbooks. Remember, these were old Jews, for whom learning and teaching are sacred. After some discussion, ninety-one-year-old Gus, a tiny, stooped, fiercely serious Holocaust survivor, who had protested that he was already teaching once a week at a school for Jewish boys, who were far more worthy of his attentions, decided that he would tell his story in an attempt to teach these unteachables. With Gus in line, most of the others made tentative unenthusiastic commitments to the project.

I met separately with the kids several more times to introduce them to the rudiments of interviewing and some of the history they would be hearing about. We made lists of questions they might ask, and they practiced on each other. Finally it was time to start, but how to get old and young together? I decided on an introductory party: juice and cookies in the sun room. The kids would "host," and the elders would be the "guests." When I told them that they would have to greet the elders as they entered the room, seat them, and then sit down and talk, the kids asked if they could go in pairs. These strapping, brazen, street-wise "gangstas" were actually so afraid of meeting the old people socially that they were willing to unmask themselves and ask for reinforcements. I was very touched and of course agreed right away.

Party time. An old woman enters slowly. After some nudging from me, two young women go over, escort her to a seat, bring refreshments and sit down. The old woman starts the conversation, and soon the three of them are talking and laughing together. Gus enters; he is tiny and so stooped with arthritis that he walks almost bent in half. None of the kids move. Then Junior, one of the toughest, a junior high school dropout, and, by his own admission, a former thug, pulls his buddy up off his chair and the two of them go over. Others follow, and in a little while, the room is alive with triads in conversation. After the party the kids, flushed with pleasure and pride, report that they have all made dates to go to the elders' rooms the next week to start recording life stories.

And with very few hitches, the Life Stories Project went on smoothly from there. It was as simple as that. These old and young, seemingly as far apart by any measure—age, race, class, religion, education, language, tastes, whatever—fell into the roles of grandparents and grandchildren, sage and student, as naturally as if it were in their DNA. And perhaps it is.

At the beginning of the Life Stories project, the young saw *old, rich, white,* and *Jewish* and the elders saw *poor, black, uneducated,* and *lawless.* The differences were extreme, but that only points to what you will find whenever you bring young and old together. Misunderstanding, ignorance, indifference, fear, prejudice, and stereotyping are the first problems that have to be overcome in bringing old and young together. And do not be fooled by positive, sentimental stereotypes; they are only the other side of the same coin.

Language and cultural differences should not be underestimated. The young peoples' "gangsta" dress style and street faces scared the old people, whose accents and manners seemed snooty and cold to the young. With time and contact these masks evaporate, or become insignificant, but they can't be glossed early on.

Language itself can be a barrier. Words can mean or connote completely different thoughts, values, or even things. One day, Laura, an New York University student said, "I have to check my machine." Etta, then about ninety perked up and said, "Sewing machine?" She grew up on the Lower East Side in a time when her family's survival depended on a treasured pedal-driven sewing machine, which was always referred to as "the machine." Laura learned some history that day, and Etta found out something about youth culture and social change. Recently, working on fairy tales and the iconic images they teach us, we had an almost tense exchange around the word *girl.* Young women in 2003 have no problem calling each other *girl,* as in "my girls," or "You go, girl." The elder women, products of first wave feminism, can barely stand it. As one said, "I would rather cut off my arm than refer to anyone over the age of twelve as a girl." And she rattled off a list of wittily regenderized terms she and her friends had compiled in the 1970s: *personagement* (instead of *management*), *penpersonship* (*penmanship*), *Fu Person Chu,* and *personage à trois.*

The great lubricant of multigenerational collaboration is what one scholar called "the unbreakable links between old and young."[6] Once they actually get together, relationships develop quickly, as if responding to a deep hunger. And within this hunger lie opportunities to

Figure 1–1. Aaron Lorenz and Molly Seif in *Lookin' Good: A Follies*, set by Tine Kindermann. Photograph by Fran Kaufman.

teach and learn; to have life stories preserved, remembered, and passed on; to ease loneliness and isolation. All of these and more make these projects work more often than not.

> One day, Junior reported that Gus had taught him a new word: *artisan*. How did *artisan* come up? I asked. He told me he had asked Gus what he and his friends did for fun as kids in his small town in Germany. Gus said that they went to watch the artisans in their shops. And then Gus asked, "*Artisan*, is that a word in English?" Junior said, "No," he had never heard of it. But Gus wanted to check, so he pulled out a dictionary and sure enough, there it was. Junior was surprised and delighted that Gus knew more English than he did, even though he learned English late in life and still spoke with such a thick accent. Later, Gus sought me out to tell the same story, and again it was the delight in having taught something that shone through. Unintentionally, almost unconsciously, these two had fallen into the timeless roles of sage and student, and found it deeply deeply satisfying.

Junior came to love Gus. And through loving Gus, *old, rich, white,* and *Jewish* were transformed for him in the larger world as well. And the same was true for Gus in relation to *young, African American,* and *uneducated.*

This was an extreme case in terms of the differences; it might seem easier if young and old were of the same race, religion, class, language, and so on, but I have not found that to be true. Even if old and young are close in the ways we think make a difference—religion, race, class—they will still be awkward, shy, and distant, and treat each other with kid gloves at first.

Roots & Branches

After a couple of years of life stories work, I became frustrated by its limitations. The telling and recording of life stories fostered intense and powerful encounters between old and young and convinced me of the hunger for contact in both generations. But I was also aware of the limitations of the process. I had an archive of hundreds of audiotapes (some of which had been shared with families) and a couple of anthologies, but a lot was missing. Most of the tapes were never listened to. They were just too long, and much of what was on them was frankly boring—most of us aren't gifted storytellers. So, after such promising starts, everything seemed to come to a dead end. Some more artful way of presenting the stories was needed. And there were several other elements, too, either missing or misdirected.

First the relationships were too short. Everyone wanted to go on, but the vast majority of interviews ran out of gas after three or four sessions. The elders wanted the young ones to keep visiting, but with rare exceptions, they didn't. They were too busy; their lives moved on; they had full social lives; and they were still young enough to think that people are replaceable.

Second, the storyteller/interviewer relationship was limited to one basic activity. The young person interviewed the elder and the elder told stories. Informally, a lot else happened—the elders would ask questions or teach the young one knitting or history, and sometimes they invented other activities like window shopping together or going to the movies. And that convinced me of the hunger for a broader forum.

Something more lasting was needed; something with more incentive to continue, that was more collaborative, in which roles could change, to which each individual and each age group could bring their particular strengths; something that engaged young and old in a common pursuit. Theater is what I knew how to do, so that's where I went.

Making theater would keep a group of old and young working together for a considerable period of time. They would get to know each other deeply, in both formal and informal settings. They would work toward a common goal. Each would play many different roles, both as actors and within the group—improvising, telling stories, acting, rehearsing, traveling to performances, eating, dressing, making up, and going on stage together. They would laugh together, learn together, experience each other as colleagues. They would inevitably come to see one another as individuals. And their stories and experience could be communicated to others through performance.

Sounds like a good idea, doesn't it? Well, everyone I approached thought so, but it still took four years to get started. Everyone agreed that generational segregation is a bad thing, that something should be done, and doing theater or other arts together was a great idea. But for four years I could not find one institution where we could initiate such a program. Sometimes it was logistics: the old came to the center in the morning, the young in the afternoon. There were insurance issues. There were funding issues—no one at that point was funding multigenerational programs, it was either young or old. There were turf issues— who would take on the extra work of administering the program, and whose program would get credit? The issues went on and on. So many doors slammed in my face that it sounded like a Gene Krupa solo.

Then I got a call from Howard Pflanzer, a playwright who had started a senior theater group at a senior center on the Upper West Side of Manhattan. Howard wanted me to help develop and direct a play with the group. I did and fell in love. The next year, 1990, professor Jan Cohen Cruz of NYU's Tisch School of the Arts arranged for students in her Community-Based Theater class to receive credit for working with what soon became Roots&Branches.

Logistics

In 1996, choreographer Risa Jaroslow and I started out on a two-year journey called *Encounters at the Border*. Our plan was to bring together old and young people from the many nationalities who lived on the Lower East Side of New York—Chinese, Caribbean, Puerto Rican, Central American, Russian, Filipino, African American, Jewish, Italian, and

Figure 1–2. *Encounters at the Border*, co-directed by Risa Jaroslow and Arthur Strimling at Lincoln Center Out of Doors (1997). From left to right: Ofelia Rodriguez, Yim Chin, Melissa Santiago, Robert Sorrentino, David Dinolfo, Ida Harnden (hidden), Mercedes Ruiz, Mary Auyung, Wei Du Ho. Photograph by Tom Brazil.

more. The Lower East Side is still the hot center of the American not-so-melting pot, and we planned workshops in which they would share their lives in story and movement, and then create a performance. The Nathan Cummings Foundation funded us generously, and we went to several of the grand old Settlement Houses with our plan.

As when I was trying to start an intergenerational theater, everyone we talked to loved the idea and wanted to cooperate—to recruit from the many programs each agency ran for the different age and nationality groups. But then we ran into a fundamental unintended outcome of age- and nationality-oriented service programs. Each program had its own funding, its own administration, and its own clientele. And sharing clientele with *Encounters at the Border* could mean that they might participate less in your program, which could lead to loss of funding. We ended up having to do some pretty heavy politicking to get participants for our workshops.

As long as funding streams are aimed at specific age and nationality groups, and not at crossfertilization, intergenerational programs will run into road blocks.

Intergenerational theater involves different agencies as well as different age groups. This section introduces some of the types of agencies and personnel with which you will likely be working. Since the recruitment and holding issues are very different for old and young, we will deal with them separately.

Elders

To recruit seniors you can go to the mountain or bring the mountain to you. You can recruit at senior centers or residences where the seniors are. Or, you can do outreach in the larger community for a class or theater group to be established at a community center, such as a Y or community center, or a college or university that offers classes for nonmatriculated adults. Some universities now have senior theater programs, or offer classes for seniors that include fairly extensive theater offerings. In any case, make sure there is also a younger community in the area from which you can recruit.

Going to the Mountain   Most states and many cities now have departments for the aging that can provide lists of senior facilities. In addition, many religious institutions and charities, such as Catholic Charities or the United Jewish Appeal, fund and administer senior centers and residences.

Senior centers, as the name implies, are places where elderly people who live in the neighborhood can gather. Often, inexpensive nourishing lunches, and sometimes breakfasts are served. Most also offer other activities before and after lunch, including classes and study groups, exercise, group outings, as well as cards, pool, and other recreational activities.

If you have never been in a senior center you are in for a vivid experience. The place may seem unprepossessing, even depressing, and the elders even more so. But hang in there. Here's a description of the center where Roots&Branches started:

> The center is in the basement of a synagogue. A big gloomy room, the social workers have to struggle to create a cheerful atmosphere. The seniors come early—this is their community, their village, their shtetl. An elderly volunteer, tight-lipped, battleship-bosomed, collects fifty cents from each and hands each a number

handwritten on cardboard in large digits, so that even the near-blind can read, and encased in ancient, finger-greasy plastic.

They take the number to a table, making sure to get their own seat with their own friends. This is very important to them; most live alone, far from family, and for them this daily dose of socializing may be more important than the cheap lunch. I have seen otherwise dignified people throw plates of spaghetti at each other over a seat at a table.

Some write their number on the paper placemat and go off—whence the fights—to paint or dance or listen to a lecture on the Middle East or the opera. Near the front, two women schmooze while they wrap plastic-ware in paper napkins and make neat piles beside little cups of applesauce and bread slices individually sealed in cellophane. Others talk in small groups, read, or just sit, snoozing, or guarding nests of numbered placemats. They look sullen in repose—perhaps they are, or maybe it's just the droop of aged flesh.

These old folks are not cute. They don't fit the Golden Girls TV image of old people. Nor are they the blue-haired ladies and yellow-jacketed gentlemen of the suburbs. Their clothes are not new; their bodies sag, spread, and bend; bad wigs and garish slashes of lipstick or rouge abound, and the men just tend to look seedy. Some have simply stopped taking care of themselves, they don't even brush their teeth anymore. These are the ones who have lost everyone who cared how they dress, or smell, or if they are alone, or even alive. These are the ones who spurn new friendships—perhaps the pain of chancing another loss is just too great.

Lunch starts promptly at twelve—and woe to the eager lecturer who tries to keep his class a few minutes late to share one more gem. From ten minutes 'til, he or she will be speaking into an increasing shuffle of chairs and feet, until by two minutes of, even the most devoted have decamped for the lunch room. These old ones love culture, but their priorities are clear. Lunch comes first!

Given this eagerness and the well-known willingness of the elderly to ignore decorum, it is essential that the serving of the lunches follow a strict regimen. The ticket lady stands up front

with a microphone calling out numbers, like the flight atten-
dant when you board a plane: "Up to 15 . . . up to 30 . . . ," and
the old ones line up. Each receives a tray with a segmented Sty-
rofoam dish—sections for meat, vegetables, salad, and dessert.
Usually there are also a small cup of canned fruit, fresh fruit,
bread, a container of milk, and coffee or tea. Many take the
bread, milk, and fruit home, or if they don't want something,
trade, or perform small acts of charity—Sam gives his milk to
Minna, who has a cat.

The menus vary over the week: meatloaf, fish, spaghetti, stew,
and the big draw, chicken. By far the most people show up on
"chicken day." (There are several senior centers in the neighborhood, and some people actually follow the chicken from one
center to another over the course of a week.) Like any performer
I want a big audience, so I always try to schedule my visits on
chicken day.

Senior centers are generally administered by professionals, trained
in group or social work. These directors are heroically overworked and
underpaid, so one needs to approach them with well-thought out
plans that demand minimal effort and time from them. Some have
funds to pay activity leaders, but the fees are always modest, far below
market value, and not even on the scale of a living wage. They are not
likely to have funds for production or other costs. Look for a center
that has not only a general purpose room, but also classrooms or other
spaces where your group can meet in some privacy and quiet. Or, you
can do as Roots&Branches does and meet in the general purpose area
late in the afternoon, when the other seniors have left.

Residential facilities include nursing homes, where a significant
percentage of the residents need continuing medical care. While theater is certainly possible and salutary with such groups, you face physical and psychological issues that will limit what you can do. I don't
recommend such facilities for intergenerational theater. Art projects
or interview projects where young people do the active work, under
guidance and input from the elders, would work better.

The trend in retirement facilities is toward assisted living, in which
several levels of care are offered. Healthy residents live independently

in their own apartments. Assisted living facilities generally offer a wide range of activities for their residents, and might very well be open to acting and theater classes that lead toward an intergenerational program. Staff at these facilities generally includes an activities director in charge of programs. If not, approach the director of the facility.

Bringing the Mountain With the vast increase in healthy retired people with adequate incomes, there has been a parallel increase in offerings for seniors at colleges, universities, and community agencies like Ys and community centers. Since these institutions also specialize in programs for children, adolescents, college, and graduate students, they would seem to be ideal grounds for intergenerational programming. Unfortunately, they aren't, at least not yet. Very often there are difficult bureaucratic obstacles. Programs are developed along age group lines—day care, after school, health club for adults, senior classes and activities—and funding, insurance, administration, and staff are all set up to provide services separately.

So these institutions can be excellent places for theater classes and even performing groups, as long as they are aimed at the age cadres already established. In general, administrators and boards of directors love the idea of intergenerational programming, but have difficulty cutting through all the bureaucracy, personalities, insurance issues, and so on. Still, there are movements toward changing these established patterns, and if you are patient, you could end up with a real breakthrough.

Children younger than high school age work with elders better in one of the other two models described in the introduction—mentoring by the elders and/or service by the young. I helped create a program that combined the two in which a group of Russian émigré elders told their stories to junior high students, who then made a combination photo show and play, telling the stories of the elders. The school, the parents, the whole community center where the elders congregated came to see the photos and the play. The elders were honored and deeply moved to have their stories celebrated publicly. The kids learned some recent history from those who lived it, and more important made that history their own through the process of putting together a photo show with transcribed text from the interviews under each photo, and then writing, rehearsing, and successfully performing their play based on the transcripts before a large delighted audience. In Roots&Branches, everyone is potentially an equal collaborator, an equal contributor. The younger members (age 18–30) are trained actors with agile bodies and sophisticated skills. We need young people who have a lot to bring to the table, including their own stories. Their stories differ because they are still so much in a process of unfolding. While the elders also have unfolding stories, they have a lot more old stories, however unresolved they may be.

College-age people offer the potential for deep bonding. Most are away from home, often for the first time. Acting can be a competitive and isolating profession, even while in school. So they come with hunger for acceptance, affection, understanding—grandparenting. They don't usually say so, even to themselves at first. Usually they come in thinking that they are going to help these old people, whom they imagine to be lonely, frail, and needy (see the scene at the opening of this chapter). But it doesn't take long, maybe five or six meetings before it is obvious that they are more dependant on this community than the elders, who have stable lives, reasonably good health, family, friends, and rather full schedules.

The undergraduate students we include get credit for participating in Roots&Branches. Branches who are out of school receive small stipends or are employed leading workshops. High School students need to be under the supervision of a teacher or a program that assures their attendance.

A wide range of ages among the younger group has not worked well for us. When we tried including some thirteen- to fifteen-year-olds in with the nineteen- to thirty-year-olds, the ease of communication that we have always succeeded in building broke down somewhat. The older kids censored themselves on behalf of the younger ones, and the younger ones were intimidated and awed by these cool, wild, free college kids. One fall, a talented thirteen-year-old came to a few workshops, enjoyed them and said she wanted to join. But she was curious about what our plays were like. We had a lovely scene from the previous year's play (see the scene from *Béçoming Åmèriçañ* in the Anthology, p. 164), in which three teen-age girls sit on a stoop in the 1930s and talk about sex, menstruation, parents, and other *girl* topics. The scene had been improvised and performed by a Branch and two Roots, and I thought the part of the most innocent of the three (actually created by eighty-year old Ida) was perfect for this girl. "Great," I thought, "She'll really relate to this." So I set up a cold reading in workshop with her in the part. Well, the poor thing freaked at the subject matter and frank language, and the next day I got a call from her mother saying she wouldn't be back. For the umpteenth time, I had to relearn the lesson about the difference between remembering an experience and actually living it. So keep your young cadre within age ranges that communicate well with each other, who have similar issues, styles, obsessions, and acceptable topics of conversation.

The age range of the younger kids will influence the content of your plays more than anything else. That's simply because the elders are more flexible in this regard. They have all been ages ten, fifteen, nineteen, or twenty-five. They can relate in essential personal ways to the world of the young.

And the issues elders face in their lives relate to almost any of the issues with which kids are dealing. All kids, for example, wrestle with independence and dependence. They want and need to be free of parental control, but they fear losing the protection, love, and support they also need. It is, however, a very different struggle for a high school girl living at home than for her older sister living for the first time away from home. So the dialogue about independence and freedom would be quite different. Elders, too, face issues of independence—physical, financial, and spiritual. The struggle to maintain or redefine independence in the face of these challenges is a major issue, and on at least one important level, it is the same as the one the younger ones face: how to sustain a sense of autonomy in the face of your real limitations and the desire and need of others to make decisions for you.

Where and When to Meet

Logistics are likely to control a lot of this decision. Maybe there is an elementary school near an assisted living facility, and both institutions are eager to get something going between the two communities, so there you are. Or you are hired to teach an arts class for seniors at a community center that also has after-school youth programming, so you look to build interest in something intergenerational within the institution. There are many scenarios. In general, it helps to have something established within the community you are most connected to, and then bring the elders or the kids in later.

Schools and Other Places

Schools and other youth-centered communities are generally not set up for elders—too many stairs, not enough elevators, and so on. And even if that problem can be surmounted it would be dangerous to have elders in the building when a lot of kids are around. In theory it would be possible, but be careful to make arrangements for the seniors to be escorted in and out if other kids are in the building when they are there. And be sure the school is insured to cover such a program.

Neutral Space

A third possibility is to meet in a place that doesn't center on either age group. A theater for example. Many theaters have times during the day when space is available, and are looking for educational and other programs to sponsor—they can be sources of funding and community outreach.

So look around in your community. Perhaps there is a theater, museum, or other cultural institution, or something completely outside the arts, that has space when you need it, and has something to gain from your being there. But keep reading, because there are going to be steps to take before your first intergenerational workshop even if you find the perfect sponsor.

What Kind of Space?

What sort of space do you need for your workshops? First of all there must be access. Many seniors either can't or find it very hard to climb stairs—it's one of the hardest activities—so make sure there is a ground level entrance and an elevator if you are to be above the first floor. You need accessible bathrooms and water fountains. It may be essential to be able to bring in food—juice or water, cookies, and so on—because many elders must eat at regular intervals.

The workshop space must be both large enough for the group to move around in, to sit in a circle or in small groups, to be audience and performers, and also private enough for intimacy to develop.

You will need enough chairs for the group to sit in a circle, plus a few more for props. Don't accept desks. They separate people and make communication and intimacy much harder. If you have other props and costumes, make sure you have secure storage or your nice scarf or hat will end up in the senior center rummage sale—this happened to us. You also need to be able to rearrange the space: to move the chairs out of the way for movement work and improvisations; to create a performing space with the seats arranged as an audience, and so on.

Scheduling

Roots&Branches workshops are two-and-a-half hours long, once or twice a week. The minimum I could imagine for a workshop would be an hour and a half. Later we'll cover the content of workshops, but for now make sure you have enough time for people to meet and greet, warm up, and then play.

I used to think that workshops had to be in the morning, because that is the time when most seniors are at their best. But circumstances forced us to move to late afternoon, and, after the inevitable grumbling, the seniors adjusted superbly. They changed their schedules around, made sure to take it easy on the days we met, and the work hasn't suffered.

Retired peoples' schedules are relatively flexible, so you may be more controlled by the availability of the young people and by the schedules of the site. If you are at a senior center, mornings are good, but for that reason you may be competing with other activities, which will pull people away and perhaps limit access to the best space. The other problem with the morning is lunch. If you meet in the time before lunch is served, you will lose the last fifteen minutes or more of your time, not only because the seniors are getting hungry, but also because they want to get to the lunch room early enough to make sure they get their own seats at their own tables with their own friends. This is very important to them and no amount of reasoning, cajoling, intimidating, or anything else can change it. I have a theory that if the Messiah showed up at a senior center in a blaze of glory, no one would give her the slightest attention until after lunch.

Site Staff Support

As I said, the administrators you will be dealing with are busy, but they also tend to be supportive of arts programs. And you will need their support on a continuing basis to avoid competing activities that pre-empt the workshops, a quiet private space, storage, and so on. Senior center directors, in my experience, welcome the presence of young people. If the seniors are going to a school or a theater, you will need support from the security and custodial staffs to make sure that they get in and out safely. And, in general, administration can help to make your presence known and welcome throughout the site.

Who Do You Need?

Recruiting Elders

> I was about to retire a career teaching in elementary and special needs schools and I was terrified. I was looking for something to do that would keep me alive after retirement. I didn't want to stay in anything to do with teaching, I'd had enough of that. I met Arthur at a conference where he talked about Roots& Branches, and, I flipped my wig over the group. The day I came for my interview, the elevator wasn't working. It was just before my hip operation, but I walked up three flights of stairs for the interview. I was determined. I offered to do anything, just so I could be part of the group. And after a couple of years of helping with the newsletter and going to the workshops, lo and behold, I became an actor.[7]

Langston Hughes wrote about the agony and danger of a "dream deferred." I think he meant a dream forever deferred, a dream that can never even be pursued, much less realized. But this generation of elders has achieved something that was probably never so widespread in all of human history. It's called *retirement*. Social Security, Medicare, 401(k)s, union pensions, investments, and the revolutions in medicine and nutrition have made it possible for the vast middle class in America and other developed countries to make retirement a time to pursue deferred dreams. They may not be rich, but they have enough so they don't have to work or worry about having a roof over their heads, enough to eat, and at least basic medical care. And they have their health—we can now reasonably expect to remain healthy well into our 70s and even 80s. In Roots&Branches we have a ninety-six-year-old, and have had several who could keep up with our rather grueling schedule well into their eighties. This extended leisure time is unprecedented in human history, and we are only beginning to learn how to use it well, for ourselves and for the good of our communities and society as a whole.

So, many seniors harbor a dream, a dream they may have carried quietly, desperately, for decades. As young people, they wanted to act (or write or paint or sing) but they were poor and couldn't afford the financial risks of a career in the arts. Others, particularly women, grew up in a world in which the arts were just not a proper pursuit for a young person of that generation. But now they have the means and the world has changed. It's their time and they want to grab it.

All this is to say that it should not be difficult to find seniors interested in acting. Go to any senior center or adult education program, and chances are there will already be an acting class, a play reading group, or a theater that puts on shows. Maybe all three and more. Or just put an ad in any paper read by the senior community and you will get plenty of interest. The problem is how to choose people who are right for the kind of theater you want to do and who are serious enough to stick it out for the long run. There are several considerations.

Experience is wildly overrated as a criterion. Roots&Branches has had some actors with years of professional experience, even entire careers in the theater. They tend not to work out, because in order to survive in *the business* they had to develop and hone a *schtick*, a character and a set of mannerisms that set them apart and at the same time fit some theatrical type. That's how you get hired in commercial theater. But if you have been living off schtick for decades, it's hard to change. On the other hand, we have actors who worked out well who take regular classes and have experience in community theater groups and one of our most wonderful, loyal, and creative members had a twenty-year career in vaudeville before marrying and raising a family. So, while all rules exist to be broken, on the whole I tend to steer away from *professionals*.

I do look for elders who have some "life on their backs," as Kent says in *King Lear*; people who have lived full, rich lives, who have stories to tell, and who exude character. Then I do look for that deferred dream, that longing, and finally what my mentor Joe Chaikin called "an urgency to be heard," the deep need that has to be there inside of every actor to be a focus of attention, to tell their story, to impress themselves upon the world. If those elements are there, I don't care if they have experience; I know I can teach them the acting skills they will need. The other stuff I can't teach.

Untrained actors, however, almost no matter how talented they are, do have real limitations. And one of the most important things I have learned is to work within those limitations. Generally, untrained actors can't play well very far from themselves. But if they have talent, elders really can play themselves; they have been doing it for a long time, and by now they have it down. And their selves are interesting. They are not empty vessels. They have lived; they have thought about life; they have something to say. So the trick is to intensify and theatricalize who they are.

I do not teach acting as such in Roots&Branches. As we work through the process of gathering material, the actors do a lot of improvising, storytelling, talking, and inventing. I watch very closely. I look for the theatrical essence of each actor. By this I mean what it is about them, their presence, their physique, their voice and mannerisms that can be concentrated and intensified into something that will communicate on stage. Then, when we are working on the script, I try to edit their words to bring out that essence.

The Chapter Called "Me": Profiles

The following are some brief representative sketches of old and young people who have fared well in Roots&Branches:

"I always knew from preschool when I played Santa Claus. I always wanted to be an actress," says Esther. "But no one asked me what I wanted, and it didn't matter. My problem was finding what I had to do for my mother and me to stay alive. I did get involved in a couple of pageants and puppet shows in my late teens. And then I had a family. When I retired I decided the rest of my life would be the chapter called 'Me.' I would explore all the things I never could before. I no longer had to worry about rent and food, because I had a pension and Social Security. This is the best period of my life because I can give in to what I want to do."

Michaela came to Roots&Branches with community theater and professional experience. "Someone told me about an ad in the paper. I wanted to get my bones going again. I missed the joy of working on something and getting better. I wanted to do something creative that I enjoyed with a great deal of passion." Michaela values the group and the multigenerational agenda, but her core value is theater, and when the work is not challenging or interesting enough she will be the first to say so.

Richard had a long career in the technical end of the film and television industries. When he retired, he went for the other side of the camera, working often as an extra on movies and television shows, and performing in a good community theater in Chelsea. At first, Roots&Branches was "steady work" while Richard waited for the next extra job. In discussions he was lively and engaged, and his long union activism produced some good tales of injustice and struggle. But telling personal stories made Richard uncomfortable, and he kept somewhat separate from the group. Then one day he came in looking down and when someone gently asked him what was wrong, he let out that his cat had died. Everyone was immediately sympathetic and that seemed to win him over. His stories didn't necessarily become more personal, but he accepted and affirmed the community aspect of Roots&Branches, and he continued in the group for several years until his health faltered.

Sam had harbored a dream for decades. "I wanted to be an actor for as long as I could remember, but, coming from a poor family like I did, it was just too risky. I had to go make a living." And he did; he ran a successful art supply store, raised a family, and retired comfortably. So now was his chance, and he grabbed for it. He acted in community theater and then discovered Roots&Branches.

After raising a family and working as an office clerk for many years, Selma discovered acting in a senior group at the Educational Alliance on the Lower East Side. She turned out to be good at it and eventually joined Roots&Branches. But then life turned on her; first she suffered a severe bout with cancer, and as she was recovering, her son also came down with cancer and died. Now Roots&Branches is her lifeboat. She says over and over that it is the one place where she can concentrate and truly escape her pain and enjoy herself.

Ida left home at eighteen to go on the road in vaudeville. This was the mid-1930s and nice young girls from immigrant Jewish families didn't do such things. But Ida went with her mother's blessing and made a good career for herself as a dancer and acrobat. She toured the world with USO troupes during World War II, and after the war, she married a GI. For the next forty years she was a wife, mother, and office worker. Now she was a widow with grown children, and Roots&Branches became her way back to her first love.

Young

Chazz was a directing major at NYU. She affected a tough mein with hennaed hair and a ring in her nose. Full of confidence, transgressive by temperament and esthetic, she was a provocateur and a truth teller. But behind the hard exterior was a deeply loving connection to others; she is a genuinely charismatic character. Chazz joined Roots&Branches because of her grandfather; at sixteen, she cared for him when he was in the hospital, very ill. Every day for months, she helped him dress and eat and took him for walks. Then she left for college, and a few months later her mother called to say that he was at the end, past recovery, but hanging on, and a decision had to made about "pulling the plug." "You knew him best, and he loved you most," her mother told her, "So it's your decision." Chazz knew her grandfather would want the plug pulled, and she made the decision. But she was furious that the responsibility had been dumped on her teenage shoulders. This story became part of the play that year. Chazz stayed with the group for three years, co-directed a piece for us, and set a pattern of Branches staying with us after graduation and developing skills that they carry into their professional careers.

Dera, on the other hand, had never been around seniors. "I'm afraid of old people," she said when I first met her, "They creep me out. So I want to see if I can get over that. I think I missed something by not having grandparents." Dera, who is an extrovert to the core, got over her fears quickly and soon was telling the group some of her most intimate secrets. The elder women did become her surrogate grandmothers; she went out to dinner with several of them almost every week, and they helped her through some rather shaky times.

Chazz and Dera are poles of the spectrum of why young people come to us—from intense relationships with grandparents or other elders to complete unfamiliarity. In both and all along the spectrum, however, there is a yearning, a sense that the grandparent/grandchild connection is special, and a belief that there is something to be learned from being around elders. At first, this tends to be sentimental—a desire to help people they imagine needing their help, and some array of stereotypical assumptions about the elderly. These dissolve quickly as they are confronted with the power and individuality of our Roots.

2

First Meetings

Excerpt from *I Am Acting My Age!*

The setting is a park. The Roots enter slowly alone or in pairs and sit on benches; #1 and 2 are together, as are 5 and 6. #7 is uncomfortably sharing a bench with #5 and 6. The Branches enter and sit in a group on the ground, with subdivisions into couples or friends. There is a long silence during which the two groups eye each other and whisper among themselves. Then . . .

SENIOR 1: They dress like prostitutes
SENIOR 2: You're telling me
SENIOR 1: No wonder there is so much rape
SENIOR 2: You're telling me
SENIOR 1: The girls look like boys
SENIOR 2: You're telling me
SENIOR 3: They're always asking for money
SENIOR 4: They never call, they never write
SENIOR 5: Only the young are beautiful
SENIOR 6: They're so fresh and energetic
SENIOR 5: And full of hope and life

JUNIOR 1: They're so cute
JUNIOR 2: They're so wise
JUNIOR 1: They're inspiring
JUNIOR 3: They always take the good benches in the park
JUNIOR 4: And sit on them all day
JUNIOR 5: They're always complaining
JUNIOR 6: Aches and pains, aches and pains
JUNIOR 2: They don't want to try anything new

JUNIOR 1: They're stingy

JUNIOR 2: They never throw things away

JUNIOR 1: They're always saving rubber bands and ties for garbage

SENIOR 1: So they invite me for Passover and who do you think winds up in the kitchen doing all the cooking?

SENIOR 2: You're telling me

SENIOR 1: A mother can bring up ten children, but ten children can't take care of one mother

SENIOR 2: You're telling me

SENIOR 4: They never call, they never write

JUNIOR 3: They say the same thing over and over again

SENIOR 4: They never call, they never write

JUNIOR 1: Their lives were more interesting

SENIOR 5: Their lives are more interesting

JUNIOR 4: They never like who you date

JUNIOR 2: They try to fix you up with doctors

JUNIOR 1: Lawyers

JUNIOR 4: Nerds

SENIOR 3: When I was their age, I supported my grandfather. Now I'm supporting them

SENIOR 1: They think they're such individuals, and then they all have to wear the same kind of sneakers

SENIOR 2: You're telling me

JUNIOR 4: They hate our clothes

JUNIOR 1: They hate our music

SENIOR 3: To have Madonna as a role model is pretty, pretty sad

SENIOR 4: They never call, they never write

JUNIOR 5: They don't listen

SENIOR 5: They don't listen

JUNIOR 6: They only want to tell their own stories

SENIOR 1: They only want to tell their own stories

JUNIOR 4: They gossip

SENIOR 4: They gossip

JUNIOR 5: They make you feel guilty

SENIOR 4: They never call

JUNIOR 3: Guilty

SENIOR 4: They never write

JUNIOR 4: Guilty

Fast.

JUNIOR 6: They go to bed early

JUNIOR 3: They're wrinkled

JUNIOR 4: They smell

JUNIOR 5: They're all short

JUNIOR 4: They're deaf

JUNIOR 1: They always stare at you

JUNIOR 2: Old men are dirty and horny

SENIOR 1: They're always in a hurry

SENIOR 2: You're telling me

SENIOR 1: They bring eleven items to the ten item checkout

SENIOR 2: You're telling me

SENIOR 3: Their clothes don't match

JUNIOR 2: They still use aerosol hairspray

SENIOR 5: They wear black, black, black

JUNIOR 3: When they reach 60, they enter the age of polyester

JUNIOR 4: They have weird hairdos

SENIOR 1: They have weird hairdos

SENIOR 2: You're telling me

SENIOR 6: They're so fresh and energetic

SENIOR 5: And full of hope and life

JUNIOR 1: They're so cute

JUNIOR 2: They're so wise

JUNIOR 1: They're inspiring[8]

Starting with Age Groups Separately

The scene that introduces this chapter, "The Clichés," grew out of the first intergenerational meetings, before there was such a thing as Roots&Branches. More out of fear than sense, I decided to meet separately with the two groups before getting them together.

In a room at NYU, I first did the "Imagine an eighty-year-old, then imagine yourself at eighty" exercise. Then I asked the ten or so young actors to say or act out every stereotype, cliché, or prejudice about old

45

people they had ever heard or maybe thought. It did not matter if they believed it; they could hate it, just so long as they had thought or heard it. Most young actors, particularly the *character* types, have played old people at some time or other, so right away we got a lot of hunched backs, shuffling steps, and high crackly voices. That broke the ice, and pretty soon no one was censoring anything. It was savage and hilarious, and went on for at least half an hour. When it was over, we all knew something special, almost scary, had happened. It was a kind of exorcism of the demons of our fears and prejudices. And once the demons were out in the open, raw and unashamed, we could look at them, confront them, begin to compare them to the reality of the elders we were about to meet.

The improv was so successful that I decided to try the same thing with the old people—that is, have them act out clichés and stereotypes about twenty-year-olds. This time it started slowly because they seemed to be doing sentimental memories of themselves as twenty-year-olds. The images were idealized, sweet, and boring. So I stopped and said, "No, I meant twenty-year-olds of today." Then the floodgates opened. It was just as biting and funny as the kids had been.

I couldn't wait to bring the two groups together and have them act out their clichés for each other. But it seemed prudent for them get to know each other a little first. So after a couple of separate sessions, I brought the two groups together for the first time. At this point everyone was positive about the idea of intergenerational workshops, and eager to meet. There is a strong sentiment in favor of this sort of thing, but it doesn't go very deep, so I couldn't count on that positiveness to carry things very far. Once the sheen wore off, would the elders begin to resent the young's attitude, and would the young start to resent the slow, opinionated elders? I decided to use a few workshops for getting acquainted before plunging into the clichés.

In a conventional production where actors are brought together to perform roles in a scripted play, it is often better that the actors not get to know one another personally, at least at first, so that personal relationships don't leak into character relationships. Ensemble-created plays are the opposite. They require intimacy; the actors have to reach into themselves for the material that will become the play, and that requires a different kind of trust and openness in the group.

46

So from the first the object is to build openness and trust. Here are a few beginning exercises we do.

Names

Pair off, old/young as much as possible, and have the pairs spread around the room so their talking won't interfere with others. Each partner tells the other a story about one of their names—first, middle, last, nickname, secret name, name they wish they had, whatever. The one who is listening, must do just that, only listen. That seemingly obvious instruction is important because many people will fall into the conversational habits of feeling the need to interject sympathetic anecdotes. The listener may ask questions to clarify or draw out more of the story, but otherwise keep yourself out of it. When the first teller is done, there is no need to comment on the story. Just go on to telling your own story. The director should tell only this part of the instructions at this point; wait to tell the next part, until after they have told their stories, to give away the game. Five minutes apiece should be plenty; three is usually enough. Note for yourself the special kind of atmosphere in the room when people are telling and listening to stories.

Once all pairs are finished, regather in the circle, and then give the next instruction: Each person will introduce their partner to the group, and tell the story the partner told. In retelling, the storytellers must stick as close as they can to what they remember; they must respect the story and the teller. You can fill in details imaginatively, but out of respect, stick close to what you recall of what you heard. And the stories can be told in any form; third person, first person as the one whose story is being told, as a character in the story who is not the teller, whatever. The person whose story is being told must listen as if it is a story about someone else, a strange and new story. They cannot correct inaccuracies and the tellers can't ask for information they're unsure about.

Giving the second part of the instructions after the stories are told allows people to listen as they normally do. If they know they will have to report, they will listen differently, take notes, clarify details for the sake of the report, not out of curiosity. They will act like reporters. One goal of the exercise is to experience firsthand how stories are transformed in the retelling.

After all the stories had been told, the group was eager to talk about the experience; I didn't have to ask. Ida expressed amazement at hearing her story told by someone else, how it was accurate but the teller emphasized parts of her story that she had never thought were important. It gave her a whole new sense of what her story meant. Matt knocked himself for what a poor listener he was; that he had hardly remembered anything, even though Molly's story was fascinating. There were several nods of agreement. Chazz said she felt self-conscious telling Muriel's story with Muriel sitting right next to her, but Muriel said it made her feel like a figure out of a novel or a myth to hear her story told. She loved it. Sam, the intellectual of the group, brought up the power of names, how once you knew someone's name and the story attached to it, you knew something deep about them. Others talked about how styles in names change, how names like Muriel, Minna, Ida, Esther, Sam, and Bernie had gone out of fashion and now Jessica and Jennifer were really in, while Michaela and Chazz were always unique.

Walking

After the Names exercise I wanted to get people on their feet and interacting in nonverbal ways. We started just walking around the space, exploring it; then walking very slow, then fast, then in patterns, like going through the center and touching a wall. At this point I give the instruction to go for the open space, that is, if someone is in your path, change direction and go for the open space. I sped this up, so they would have to be very watchful of each other. Then I laid out some flowers I had brought in different places on the floor and told them to make paths around them. Then to follow someone without their knowing it. Then to meet each other's eyes and greet silently, then walk in pairs, changing partners on signals. There are infinite possibilities of walking play; all serve to make the actors comfortable in the space and more aware of each other. In the discussion, tall, frail Minna said she was afraid that one of the young people would not notice her and knock her over, but as it went on she saw how observant and careful and graceful they were and stopped worrying, at least about that.

Mirrors

There are many versions of Mirrors; here's the one I use. Partner off, old and young. Partners stand about three feet apart, facing each other, standing in a neutral position, and looking into each others' eyes. Often this will make beginners uneasy, and there will be giggling, comments, even wisecracks. Let it go a bit, then emphasize that this is a silent exercise, and comments will distract not only you, but others around you. Once things settle, have partners agree on a leader. Then the leader moves and the other *mirrors* the movement as precisely and simultaneously as possible. It helps to demonstrate with an experienced partner, so beginners get the example of simple, predictable, slow movements to begin with, and gradually push the limits. Emphasize that the goal is perfect mirrors, so an outsider couldn't tell who was leading and who was mirroring. Like the famous Marx brothers scene. This means that the leader is responsible for creating movements that can be mirrored. She must be constantly sensitive to her partner, moving smoothly, keeping everything within peripheral vision range, avoiding jerky and unpredictable movements, and so on. After a few minutes, call *Switch*, so leader becomes mirror and vice-versa, and keep switching at shorter intervals. Once the mirror is really working, have them do it without a leader, and see what happens. Then have people switch partners, several times, sometimes playing with someone your own age, sometimes intergenerationally.

Afterward, Chazz remarked on how individual and expressive any movement is on each old person, much more so than the young. Yes, they couldn't move as fast or agilely as the young, but what each one did was totally different from what any other did. She said it's like they have naturally what her teachers at NYU were always harping on; to express your uniqueness. It was as if they couldn't help but express their uniqueness. Samantha said she started out treating the elders like eggs, and was surprised and delighted at how far they would go. Sam said he was in love with all the young people, overwhelmed by their beauty and grace, and grateful that they were so respectful of his limitations.

Statues

This exercise moves things into the realm of touch and taking and giving weight. Like Mirrors, there are many versions of Statues, and again any of them can work. The idea is to plan with the focus on intergenerational experience in mind. We generally start in pairs, and the sculptor shapes the statue into a pose, gently moving arms, head, legs,

Figure 2–1. Selma Wernick and Sara Stock-Mayo in a movement improvisation during a workshop for *Encounters at the Border*. Photograph by Fran Kaufman.

torso, fingers, even face. Then the sculptor assumes the pose to let the statue know that it is her turn to become the sculptor. After a few rounds, switch partners, and then add the rule that now you cannot use your hands to sculpt; you have to use your head, face, shoulders, arms, torso, hips, legs, knees, and feet and whatever else, but not your hands. That makes it more sensual and imaginative.

By the time we had been through these games, the actors felt more at ease with each other and kind of infatuated with the fact of the group. They felt privileged to be there. It seemed time to cut through the sentimentality a bit.

So, I asked them to act out their clichés for each other. The elders stood against one wall and the young against the opposite. The center was the playing space. I told them anyone could go. No one moved. They were all afraid of hurting each others' feelings. I find that this is a good time to wait; to let the group live with the tension and see what happens. Finally Matt, the boldest, bent himself into a particularly grotesque caricature of a dirty old man walking all bent over and dim-eyed and croaking about pretty girls. It was as if by car-rying it too far he was taking the edge off, letting them know he didn't really mean it. Molly, eighty-five and stick straight, yelled, "I don't walk like that," and then did a slouchy young person pushing and yelling on the subway. And we were off. Everyone censored a bit from what had gone on separately, but it still got pretty edgy. Even-tually, they started correcting each other, old adding clichés about old and young about young. By the end we knew we had moved to a new level. The demons were out in the air again; we knew that even though the predominant feelings in the room were affection, caring, and respect, there was also an unavoidable dark side, a shadow world that had to be explored as well.

Richard, a retired union man and political activist, brought up the way that this shadow world plays itself out in the political arena. At that time (about 1990) there was a lot of journalism and political talk about *generational equity*. It had been started as a way of attack-ing Social Security, Medicare, and other benefits for the elderly. The idea was that the "greedy geezers" were robbing the young of their present income (through Social Security taxes) and future retire-ment, because of dire predictions about the Social Security funds running out by 2002 or 2010, or whenever they would be ready for it. On the other hand, the argument went, elders were being squeezed by taxes for schools, and why should they care because they wouldn't be around to reap the benefits when these educated young-sters grew up? Fortunately the movement faded rather quickly, but there was some pretty sensational and ugly rhetoric pitting old against young. We all sensed that what we were doing was a coun-terforce to this way of thinking; that the way to build our society was for the generations to care for each other. We probably got pretty grandiose in our imaginings of what a powerful force our vision and our art could be, but at any rate we knew we were on to something, and having a good time, too.

The focus of all of these and whatever other improvs you like— group statues, machines, and so on—is to bring the group to a place of ease with other, and to begin to know each other as individuals, not just old or young people. And again, I encourage discussion between exercises. It gives a rest to those who need it, while encouraging talk about differences, similarities, what it's like to touch a frail-looking eighty-year-old or a gorgeous young man.

And each time the place of ease is reached, it needs to be disrupted. The balancing of ease and disruption is the edge that keeps the workshop cycle moving.

3

The Workshop Cycle

Excerpt from *Playing Lear*

DIRECTOR: (*As Annie, and quoting the play*) The King is coming! . . .
Music comes up (*Music; all move to Lear places*), lights down, focus
on the storyteller.
STORYTELLER: Once, in a cold and savage time, there was a kingdom,
and it was ruled by . . .
ALL: (*Bowing*) King Lear!
STORYTELLER: King Lear was old, very old, and . . .
MOLLY: Wait! I'm 95 years old; the oldest one here. Why can't I play
King Lear?
DIRECTOR: Not yet, Molly, your turn will come.
STORYTELLER: King Lear has three daughters. Goneril, the oldest;
Regan, and Cordelia (*Storyteller takes each by the hand as she names
them. Burr is still messing with her bags and arrives late as Cordelia*].
King Lear announces that he is going to retire.
LEAR: To shake all cares and business from our age,
Conferring them on younger strengths while we
Unburdened crawl toward death.
ESTHER: "While we unburdened crawl toward death?" Nice talk.
What kind of an image of retirement is that? I think we should
rewrite that. "While we enjoy our golden years." See, it's nicer
and it even fits in iambic pentameter. (*In rhythm*) While we enjoy
our golden years.
LEAR: "While we enjoy our golden years."
DIRECTOR: I don't think so. Let's stick to Shakespeare.
YVETTE: Here, here!
DIRECTOR: But, Bernie, play Lear really old and senile. He's totally
out of control in his demands.

MARCY: All he wants is a little reassurance, a little love. He is giving up everything, after all.

DIRECTOR: Well, I'm the Director, so let's try it this way, Okay? Let's go . . .

STORYTELLER: So, King Lear has a map brought in.

Bryan brings map.

And he announces . . .

LEAR: Know that we have divided in three our kingdom.

STORYTELLER: And he is going to give each daughter a share, so that . . .

BRYAN: Wait a minute. Does Lear have any sons?

DIRECTOR: No.

BRYAN: So, that's why he's turning over the country to his daughters?

DIRECTOR: Right, we're not presenting "Lear the Liberated" here.

STORYTELLER: But he does have two sons-in-law. Goneril and Regan are married.

DIRECTOR: Yes, but we don't have enough men in this group, so we're concentrating on the women.

YVETTE: Okay, then but what about a wife? A queen? Don't these girls have a mother?

DIRECTOR: There are no mothers in this play.

YVETTE: No mothers? No wonder it's a tragedy!

MICHAELA: Honey, you don't know the half of it.

DIRECTOR: Right. Okay, let's continue, and Bernie make it even more out of control.

STORYTELLER: Now, King Lear is going to give each daughter a piece of the kingdom. But first . . .

LEAR: Tell me, my daughters
Which of you shall we say doth love us most,
That we our largest bounty may extend
Where nature doth with merit challenge.
Goneril, our eldest, speak first.

GONERIL: Sir, I love you more than word can wield the matter:
Dearer than eyesight, space and liberty;
Beyond what can be valued, rich or rare;
No less than life, with grace, health, beauty, honor;

54

As much as child e'er loved or father found;
A love that makes breath poor, and speech unable.
Beyond all manner of so much I love you.

ESTHER: Wait a minute! I can't believe he's doing that. A father, a king! Forcing his daughters to grovel for what is already rightfully theirs. It's outrageous!

Goneril and Sabine come DC.

GONERIL: He always loved our sister most. You see how full of changes his age is?

SABINE: 'Tis the infirmity of his age: yet he hath ever but slenderly known himself.

YVETTE: (*Comes to them*) If there was a mother here, this would never have happened.

They go back to their places, as . . .

MICHAELA: But Goneril is no better. She's just pouring it on with a trowel.

YVETTE: The apple doesn't fall far from the tree.

CORDELIA: What shall Cordelia speak? Love, and be silent.

LEAR: Of all these bounds, even from this line to this,
With shadowy forests and with meadows riched,
With plenteous rivers and wide-skirted fields,
We make thee queen. To thee and thine be this
Perpetual. What says our second daughter,
Our dearest Regan?

REGAN: I am made of the self mettle as my sister,
And prize me at her worth. In my true heart
I find she names my very deed of love;
Only she comes too short, that I profess
Myself an enemy to all other joys
Which the most precious square of sense possesses,
And find I am alone felicitate
In your dear highness' love.

BRYAN: This is disgusting! It's unreal.

DIRECTOR: Can we just get on . . .

MARCY: But I hate hypocrisy!

YVETTE: Oh, come on; don't you flatter your family? And they flatter you, coming over on Mother's Day with flowers and "World's Greatest Grandma" T-shirts.

MARCY: And then I don't see them again for two months.

YVETTE: And don't they ever go . . .

STORYTELLER & BRYAN: Grandma, please can we have ice cream, please, we love you so much. You're the best grandma in the whole world!

YVETTE: And don't you go,

MARCY: Give me a big hug and a kiss and I'll take you to the movies.

YVETTE: Flattery, it's a song we all know well.

SABINE: And that's a song cue if I ever heard it.

DIRECTOR: Listen, I appreciate the creativity, but the play is already written. We don't have time for songs.

BRYAN: Yeah, but wait 'til you hear this. *The Song of Flattery.*

Sabine sings, joined by others.

It's an old familiar story
One that really isn't fair
There'll be something that you're needing
But your pleading
Won't get you there

So you need another tactic
Something certain not to fail
Coat your fodder or your mudder
With some budder
And you'll prevail

Sing the song of flattery
It's a tune we all know well
Though it sounds like heaven to hear
It can lead you straight to hell
Sing the song of flattery
Though the words are cheap
What you get by using them
You may get to keep

Figure 3–1. Muriel Mervis as Goneril, Sabine Auf der Heyde as Regan in *Playing Lear* (2002). Photograph by Elena Olivo.

Ha ha ha ha ha oh yeah!
Say you need a new apartment
Or your boots are wearing thin
And your wallet's even thinner
Than your dinner
Of chicken skin
There's no need to get the razors out
Trust me help is on the way
With a little book of phrases
Full of praises
You'll be okay!

Sing the song of flattery (Love your shoes!)
It's a tune we all know well (What a mind!)
Though it sounds like heaven to hear (Great haircut!)
It can lead you straight to hell (Goodness I've never seen so many
    chins on one person)
Sing a song of flattery, though the words are cheap (That must
    have cost a mint!)

What you get by using them, you may get to keep! (You're just the
    best audience ever! Olé!)
CORDELIA: Then poor Cordelia;
    And yet not so, since I am sure my love's
    More weighty than my tongue
DIRECTOR: (*To Bernie*) So, now you point to the map and say to Regan . . .
LEAR: To thee and thine hereditary ever
    Remain this ample third of our fair kingdom,
    No less in space, validity and pleasure
    Than that conferred on Goneril.
SABINE: You know, he's really just asking for love. It's like my father.
    My sister got married, and a couple of weeks later he called me.
    . . . (*Phone rings, she picks it up*) Hello?
BERNIE: (*As father on phone*) How are you, sweetheart?
SABINE: Oh, hi, Dad. I'm fine. How are you and mom? Exhausted
    from the wedding?
BERNIE: You know weddings . . . emotional. But your sister . . . I
    couldn't have given her away to a better guy.
SABINE: Yes, and I hope you and my future husband will have a good
    relationship.
BERNIE: Well, you still have a lot of time.
SABINE: Oh, sure, but I think about these things.
BERNIE: So, are you all right, so far away, in the big city?
SABINE: I'm fine.
BERNIE: You're learning a lot?
SABINE: And I'm loving it.

Pause, Bernie sighs.

SABINE: Dad, are you all right?
BERNIE: You know what, honey, I have to go now.
SABINE: No, no, no, no . . .
BERNIE: I'll call you on Sunday, okay?
SABINE: No, that's three days off. I don't like your tone of voice. Are
    you and Mom okay?
BERNIE: Your mother's fine your mother's always fine.
SABINE: What about you?
BERNIE: I'm fine. I'll talk to you Sunday.

Figure 3–2. Bernie Basescu and Sabine Auf der Heyde in *Playing Lear* (2002). Photograph by Elena Olivo.

SABINE: No, I can't wait until Sunday for you to tell me.

Long pause.

Hello?

BERNIE: Just don't forget me. Don't forget me. (*Hangs up slowly*).

Pause.

DIRECTOR: Well, if Lear treated his daughters like your father treats
　　you and your sister, I would be more sympathetic. But he's drained
　　the soul out of these sisters, and look what happens to the one
　　who has any humanity left.

LEAR: And now, our joy, our youngest, Cordelia,
　　Although our last and least, what can you say to draw
　　A third more opulent than your sisters? Speak.

CORDELIA: Nothing, my lord.

LEAR: Nothing?

CORDELIA: Nothing.

LEAR: Nothing will come of nothing. Speak again.

CORDELIA: Unhappy that I am, I cannot heave
　　My heart into my mouth. I love your majesty
　　According to my bond, no more nor less.

YVETTE: Ooh that's cold. There is no compassion for an elderly parent.

BURR: I told him I love him.

DIRECTOR: Right, that should be enough.

MICHAELA: But why can't you just say, "Oh, Daddy, you're the
　　greatest."

BURR: I tried that.

LEAR: How now, Cordelia? Mend your speech a little,
　　Lest you may mar your fortunes.

CORDELIA: Good my lord,
　　You have begot me, bred me, loved me. I
　　Return those duties back as are right fit,
　　Obey you, love you, and most honor you.
　　Why have my sisters husbands if they say
　　They love you all? Haply, when I shall wed,
　　That lord whose hand must take my plight shall carry
　　Half my love with him, half my care and duty.
　　Sure I shall never marry like my sisters,
　　To love my father all.

LEAR: But goes thy heart with this?

CORDELIA: Ay, my good lord.

LEAR: So young, and so untender?

CORDELIA: So young, my lord, and true.

LEAR: (*Enraged*)

Let it be so, thy truth then be thy dower!
For, by the sacred radiance of the sun,
I here disclaim all my paternal care,
Propinquity, and property of blood,
And as a stranger to my heart and me
Hold thee from this forever, my former daughter!

BRYAN: I can't believe a parent would banish their own daughter.

ANNIE: It happens. It happened in my family.

BRYAN: What do you mean?

ANNIE: My sister . . . no, I don't want to interrupt the rehearsal . . .

ESTHER: You can talk to us.

MARCY: What about your sister?

ANNIE: Well, she was living on her own, and one day she came home, and she went down to our father's den . . .

Esther enters as sister.

JULIE: Dad, I have to speak to you.

Annie takes on role of her father, sitting in front of TV watching a ball game. Sounds of game.

FATHER: Yeah. Yeah, what's on your mind? (*Julie sits, pause*).

JULIE: Dad. . . . I don't know how to start . . .

FATHER: You dating that jerk again?

JULIE: No, it's still Sean. I'm really serious about him.

FATHER: You know, Julie. You're a smart girl; you're my daughter. He's not going anywhere.

JULIE: But you don't know him like I do.

FATHER: I don't want to talk about this any more. You know how your mother and I feel. And if you want to go against us, that's fine. . . . But it makes me sick.

JULIE: Dad, I'm pregnant.

Silence.

Did you hear me, Dad? It's Sean's.

FATHER: How can walk into this house and look me in the face and tell me . . . this?

JULIE: Because I love you.

FATHER: You call this love?

JULIE: Nothing more, nothing less.

FATHER: You are going to have this baby, you're not going to . . .

JULIE: Yes, yes, I am going to have the baby.

FATHER: All right. But you have to turn your back on that sc . . . loser, and come back home. We will support you until you can go back to work, and then your mother will take care of the baby while you're at work. What do you say?

JULIE: Nothing. (*Pause, then Lear addresses Cordelia while Father speaks to Julie*)

FATHER & LEAR: Nothing?

JULIE & CORDELIA: Nothing.

FATHER: So young . . .

LEAR: And so untender?

JULIE & CORDELIA: (*They stand together, each facing her father*) So young, my lord, and true.

LEAR: (*Enraged*) Let it be so, thy truth then be thy dower!

FATHER: For, by the sacred radiance of the sun,
     I here disclaim all my paternal care,

LEAR: And as a stranger to my heart and me
     Hold thee from this forever,

FATHER: My former daughter.

LEAR: My former daughter.

Pause . . . Cordelia and Julie exit arm in arm.[9]

Choosing a Theme

Over the years we have worked with many themes, including work, love, independence, immigration, beauty, time, stereotypes and clichés, and generational equity. We have also started from works of literature, including *Romeo and Juliet*, *Three Sisters*, Brecht's short story "An Appalling Old Lady," *King Lear*, and fairy tales. In every case the choice was based on our sense that the theme meets three basic criteria:

1. It lends itself to our core focus on intergenerational issues and connections.
2. It has strong theatrical possibilities.
3. It is broad enough to allow for a wide range of workshop possibilities.

Obviously there are a lot of themes one could pursue. The two most common suggestions being death and whatever political issue is hot at the moment—Social Security, taxes, education, war. Topical issues are worthy topics for essays or agitprop, but they don't open up much room for improvisation, storytelling, and discussion, and death is, well . . . death. An exception on both counts was our AIDS play, *Old AIDS*, which deals with grandparents coming to terms with their beloved grandson's sexual orientation and illness. It rose not out of any consensus, but out of an improvisation proposed by Sam and Minna, two of our original elders. So ultimately AIDS became the springboard for a play about compassion and understanding between the generations.

Often it takes several workshops to settle on a theme. That doesn't mean that we just sit and talk. We keep moving from discussion to improvisation, and stories inevitably come up. Usually a consensus emerges, almost in an unspoken way. The general theme is exactly that, general. It rules nothing in or out during the workshop process, but gives us a background focus. And often the real theme doesn't emerge until much later. For example, the year we took immigration as our theme, it emerged after several weeks that all but one of our elders and several of the youngers were children of immigrants, and that there was enormous common ground between them around that experience—being torn between the old world and the new; knowing more English than their parents; and having to translate both language and culture for them. Even though the Roots were mostly Jewish and the Branches were a wide mix, including Filipino, Chicano, and Russian, the experiences were the same. So the play, *Bécoming Åmèriçañ*, focused on the second generation experience.

A Table with People

It's about 2:45 P.M., fifteen minutes before the workshop is scheduled to start. Yvette, Marcy, and Esther are sitting at one of the round tables

in the large lunchroom, eating cookies, and shmoozing. Others strag-
gle in. By 3:15 P.M. everyone is there, but the shmoozing goes on until
about 3:30 when, with some urging from David and me, the group
moves from the table to the circle of chairs in the workshop space.

This routine has never varied. It used to drive me crazy. I wanted
everyone there and ready to get started at 3:00 like professionals, so we
could get the most out of our too brief time together. But no matter
how I tried, it never happened. I tried reasoning; I tried cajoling; I
tried anger and intimidation; I tried bribery. Nothing worked. They
would always hear me out and agree that I was right, and then go right
on doing what they had always done. After a couple of years, I gave up
and joined them.

At first I was bored and impatient with what I saw as small talk, but,
for the sake of appearances, I pretended to enjoy it. Gradually my pretending got the best of me and I actually began to look forward to the
time around the table. They had me, these elder women—because it
was definitely the women who made this happen. And once I enjoyed
the shmoozing, I began to see the wisdom in it. This is the time of
coming together, developing the small intimacies that make the larger
ones of the workshop possible—building community, as the theorists
say. It's the wisdom of the kitchen table, the breaking bread and catch-
ing up. The Yiddish expression for this is *a tisch mit mentschen*, "a table
with people"; I'm sure every culture has a similar phrase. It is where we
learn about someone's struggle with a landlord; how another one's wife
is recovering from surgery; the latest installment of a romance or a battle with a sexist professor—the aches, pains, and triumphs of a week
shared around the table. It is where the visceral bond between old and
young is forged anew each week. I am eternally grateful to these
women for this teaching.

In this sense, community-based theater is fundamentally different
from professional or even amateur community theater. We are not
together solely to put on a show. Some community-based theaters—
early women's and gay theater, African American theater, theater of
the deaf—reach deep into the values and issues of their community in
order to express, to strengthen, and to affirm that community. In our
case our plays aim to evoke a sort of model community, and in order
to do that we have to build one anew each season.

So bring some cookies yourself, and don't fear allowing for some schmooze time before you get to work. There is real work going on around that table with people.

The Den Mother, the Diva, and the Adorable Daughter

Another aspect of this is the natural evolution of roles within the group—the den mother, the adorable child, the wise one (old or young), the wise guy (male or female), the diva, the clown, and so on. All groups have these roles, but in a continuing ensemble, they are very important to observe, encourage, and also sometimes break. It is most important to me to have a den mother (male or female) who loves keeping track of birthdays, deaths, illnesses, romances, who serves the social worker role that is inevitably part of such a community. Partly it shields the director from having to take on that role, but also because she is such a good confidante, she can pass on information, issues, complaints, stories, that I might not know, and need to know.[10] Everyone understands this role; there are no secrets about it, and I am quite certain that the Roots&Branches den mother also keeps a lot of necessary secrets from me, and I thank her for it (I say *she* because in my experience this role is always played by an older woman in Roots&Branches; it might be different in other groups).

The Circle: Warming Up

We begin in a circle of chairs, so those who need to sit or can't stand for long are comfortable. Our warm-ups are simple, playful, and nontechnical. The young actors are in terrific shape and the elders, having very different needs, exercise on their own. We avoid technical physical warm-ups. It's more about moving from the social space to the workspace than physical and vocal preparation.

Some of the introductory exercises have already been covered and all of these can be adapted for warm-ups. We make it a practice to do some simple massage as part of most warm-ups. For example, have everyone in the circle turn to their left, and move in enough to be within easy reach of the person in front of you. Then massage their shoulders, neck, arms, and back for a couple of minutes. Next, have everyone turn 180 degrees and massage your former massager. Everyone loves this, of course, but it goes deeper. First, because many elderly people live alone and touch no one from week to week. So a hug or massage can mean a great deal. The famous experiments by the psychologist Harry Harlow demonstrating the effects of touch, and the lack of it, on babies applies, I believe, to the elderly as well.[11]

The core of the warm-up will usually be a couple of rounds of sound and movement. In our style of sound and movement, each actor does a phrase or sound with a gesture, and the group then copies it together. We almost always choose a topic for this section that relates to the workshop of the day.

During the first few weeks of workshops, when the younger actors are still new and unfamiliar with seniors, we do the pairs and other exercises described in Chapter 2. Warm-ups generally take fifteen or twenty minutes, and by the end we are together as a working ensemble, and into the content for the day's workshop.

"Which of You Doth Love Me Most?": How Workshops Work

Life Stories, Discussion, Improvisation, and Text

These are the central elements of the Roots&Branches process. Our workshops weave from one to the other, by plan or impulse, in no set order. The pleasure principal rules. Because it's impossible to know beforehand if a particular exercise will produce anything we can use in the play, we go instead with whatever draws us in the moment. The theme and the goal of making a play are always in our minds, but toward the back. Our path is indirection and the general rule is that digression rules. I try to create a sort of orderly anarchy in our workshops in which everyone feels free to contribute openly, but no one is pressured. Some love to talk and tell stories; some almost never speak up, but blossom in improvisations. Some go right for the topic at hand, some wander in off-the-wall directions that may be paths or dead ends, but we won't know until we get there.

Which element we use to explore a particular moment, idea, or theme depends on several calculations: the kind of material we are seeking; a sense of the best way to explore that moment, idea, or theme; its dramatic potential; trial and error and, not least, blind inspiration. Often, for example, a discussion of something we read will provoke a story from someone that we decide to turn into an improv, which in turn produces more discussion and stories, and so on. We plan our workshops carefully beforehand, but the plan usually goes out the window as unexpected opportunities arise.

I'm not prescribing orderly anarchy as a necessary method for this kind of work or for ensemble creation in general. Some directors, probably most, are more orderly and intentional, and God bless you. So in order to convey our disorder, but give some useful ideas to assist your own sense of order, this chapter will describe one sequence of four workshops. Those who seek rules can find them in this description; those who seek only inspiration, will, I hope, also find plenty of that. The description is built a little from memory, but mostly from reading and rereading the transcripts.

> At a Board of Directors meeting in the spring of 2000, we opened with an "ice breaker." Before turning to business, we asked everyone to describe an intergenerational issue in their own lives. It was striking how much conflict there was in the stories, including one in which a distinguished elder member told about how his eldest son was trying to take over as head of the family. In that instant David and I looked at each other across the big board meeting table and mouthed, *"King Lear."*

It was an absurdly ambitious notion, but after ten years, the thought of exploring generational issues through the lens of maybe the greatest play ever written was irresistible to us and to some of the actors in the company. Others were dubious, but willing to give it a try.

At our first meeting we started with one of the introductory exercises already described. We concluded the warm-up with a name go 'round, in which each actor says her/his name with a gesture, and everyone repeats the name and gesture and also all the names and gestures up to that point. By the end, we knew each others' names and, having stood and moved for ten or more minutes, the elders needed to sit down.

The next exercise began our entry into the world of King Lear. But we did not start with the play. We knew that, while some actors knew the play, most had never read it, and at least one was openly hostile to Shakespeare—"Why does he have to make it so hard to understand?" So, we had to start slowly, introducing the themes before we confronted the text.

This is a more spontaneous form of the go 'round we used to learn names. In this form, anyone can speak up at any time, so actors can more readily play off each other. Gestures are not required, and the group does not repeat what was said, so the focus is on content. We do this kind of exercise often; it falls somewhere between an improv and an open discussion. In Roots&Branches though, discussions often break out in the middle of it, and we tend to let them go, and then return to the form.

The question was: What do you want to pass on to future generations, and what do you want older generations to pass on to you? The basic form is to answer in brief phrases or sentences.

> I would like to pass on to my grandchildren a sense of commitment and passion to people and things of the world.
> I want to take all my money and divide it among my progeny—I'll open a bank account for each one of them and divide all the money I have.
> I'd like to inherit my grandmother's sense of style, her lady-ness. Every piece of clothing I have that gets complimented is from her.
> To pass on my mother's energy to my grandchildren and my sense of fun to my children . . .
> To inherit even more of my nana's unshakable faith
> My mother gave me a quilt her mother made—it's all little rosettes, hundreds of them, and it's beautiful. I can't decide yet which child I trust to cherish it and keep it in the family forever.

And there are things you don't want to inherit or pass on.

> I'm thinking of my father's terrible temper. One time—I must have been twelve or thirteen—he was yelling at my mother

and the next thing I knew he threw a dozen eggs out the window. I'm really grateful that he took it out on the eggs, not my mother. I inherited his temper, except at the price of eggs today I don't throw them out the window.

Why did I have to inherit aunt Kelly's nervous stomach?

I'm so glad I didn't inherit my father's good judgment and sensibleness. It's restrictive.

I look in the mirror and I think, "How did my cousin Rosy's nose get on my face?"

I hated inheriting both parents' sarcasm. It's a curse to see everything from a sarcastic point of view.

And so on. In this little preliminary exercise, without even looking at the play, the group had raised basic issues of *King Lear* in personal ways—what is passed on and how; what's wanted, what's resented; struggles within and between generations. We were entering the terrain of the play.

The actors were charged up and, having sat for a while, were ready to get up and move again, as well as go farther into the world of the play. The next exercise took the form of a *relay improv.*

Begin with one actor (A) in the playing space. Then a second actor (B) enters, and defines the relationship by words and action. This particular improv is about legacy, so the rule is that actor B must present a situation in which she is an older generation offering a legacy, or a younger generation wanting one. The legacy can be spiritual or material, but it and the relationship must be made clear by Actor B's opening gambit. Actor A, the one first in the space, assumes the necessary role, and off they go. When the scene is played out to acceptance or rejection of the request, or an impasse, actor A leaves, B takes the stage, and a third (C) enters, presenting a new situation with new characters. Thus everyone gets to initiate a scene and respond to another's initiative. The improv ends with a scene initiated by the original actor.

A: I'm going to draw you a map.
B: Okay—why?

A: This is a map that will show you how to get to the most sacred and romantic place in our whole family. Your grandmother and I went to this place when we pledged our troth to each other. When you find the one you love you take him . . . or her . . . to this place. . . . And that's where everyone in our family pledges their troth to each other.

B: What if I want to do it differently?

A: Why would you want to do it differently?

B: Because I'm not you. So I might want to live my life differently. Is that okay?

A: Your mother and father—they went there. Your uncle and aunt—

B: Right. But does that mean I have to?

A: I don't know. But I think you'd be missing out on something. I was going to tell you to save the map, not look at it until you're ready. But maybe—it's a different time. See, my father told me to do this, and it never crossed my mind not to do it. But you're a different time.

B: Well—

A: Maybe you need to go there and see. It might even have changed. I don't know. Everything has changed.

B: Well, I will definitely check it out and let you know what I experience, okay?

A: Okay, just come back and tell me if it's still all blue out there.

B: Okay—I'll let you know if it's blue. Thank you for this. I'll keep it and I'll . . .

A: Hold on to that, okay? That's where your grandma and I pledged our troth.

A exits, C enters.

C: I just got a new apartment and all I can think when I look at my wall is how amazing it would be to have Grandma's Renoir.

B: But if Grandma sold it, it would be in a museum, we could go see it . . .

C: Grandpa bought that painting—Grandma is not gonna sell it! Wasn't there something else you want? Wasn't there something else?

B: So it's gonna fit your kitchen? So you have to have the Renoir?

C: Well, it's not just that—I mean I've been a Renoir enthusiast since many many years ago.

B: Who's not a Renoir enthusiast? You know—Grandpa always wanted me to be a lawyer—I've always taken that very much to heart and that's a lot of money . . .

C: I'm pregnant! I'm gonna have a child, so I need the painting!

B: You should get the Madonna and Child, not the Renoir!

And so on. The purely imaginary nature of this improv allowed for strong dramatic conflicts; the actors could fight fiercely without fear of revealing something intimate. So, without even looking at the text, we were well into world of the play.

Each exercise was accompanied by a good deal of discussion, so this took up the whole of our first workshop.

Having meditated together on issues of legacy, we were ready to tackle *King Lear*. But first, we warmed up by exorcizing some of our demons, positive or negative, about Shakespeare. It was analogous to the stereotypes improvs of years earlier (see p. 43). Each actor finishes a sentence beginning with the words, "Shakespeare is. . . ." The words had to be accompanied by a gesture, and then everyone repeats the line and the gesture.

"Shakespeare is . . .
An old, dead white man
Impossible to understand
Lofty yet human
Lacking subtext
Power to the people
Indecipherable
The greatest writer in the English language
Revered by actors
Groovy
Makes me stand up straight and think fast
Iambic pentameter
Such that I don't even understand the synopsis
Full of Bartlett's quotations
Poetry, psychology, and politics
"How now, my lord"
Done badly by Americans

A few rounds of this loosened everyone up, and made us aware, without discussion or argument, of the range of attitudes we were bringing to the play. As the actors returned to the circle of chairs, the air in the room was charged, and when I pulled out a stack of copies of the script, everyone was eager to get into it.

The script I handed out was a cut-down version of the great opening scene of *King Lear*, in which the aged Lear makes his daughters compete in telling him how much they love him in return for a share of the kingdom. I started by telling the story of the scene in some detail, so that everyone could follow the action even the first time they read the unfamiliar and complex language.

After making sure everyone had the story straight, we read the scene, going around the circle, each actor reading a line, or part of it if it's a long speech. No casting, little attempt at character, and no stopping; we just read. But even without a clue to the meaning of many words and phrases, the actors readily latched on to the rhythm and much of the intention and feeling behind the gaudy language. By the end of the scene, everyone was exhilarated and eager to read it again.

This time, however, we stopped at almost every line to define words and search for meaning—what does Lear mean by "our darker purpose"; what is a "square of sense"; and who were "the barbarous Scythians" anyway? Inevitably, questions of definition led to discussions of character and relationship. And, in Roots&Branches, that inevitably leads to stories about how we have responded to similar conflicts. So Lear's "while we unburdened crawl toward death," provoked this from ninety-five-year-old Molly:

MOLLY: I'm not crawling to my grave. I have two daughters, and in my will I want everyone to come to the house and choose what they want. Then I split my "great wealth" in half. The point is that I'm very anxious to do what is best for them. I don't say to them, "Which one of you loves me more?" I don't care if they love me. Let them hate me. I'm concerned with them.

And the flattery contest received some lively responses from the younger women.

CINDY: I know that my father will do something in the end, but he

makes me work for it because he's the financial head of the family.
JOYE: My mother will buy me $500 worth of clothes, and when we're
at the register and she has her credit card out about to pay, she
will say, "Isn't it nice that I'm not one of those mothers who only
buys you clothes at Christmas." Then I'm forced to respond, "Yes,
mother, it is."

Joye's shopping story stuck in my mind for months. It's a perfect
example on a domestic level of the cosmic manipulation by Lear.
Eventually we set it up as an improvisation, which developed into an
important scene in the play. But now was not the time for that.

Our focus was on getting into the scene and using whatever personal
examples came up as aid to that end. All this happened pretty sponta-
neously as we moved through the scene. Discussions about the meaning of a line or moment demand examples to back up a point, and often
examples come in the form of stories from our own lives. Once we
have, in a sense, domesticated the text, we are freed to go deeper.

A wonderful moment happened during this reading/discussion, a
pure example of the power and usefulness of digression. We're talking
about Cordelia, and suddenly Yvette bursts out, "There is no mention
anywhere in the play about mothers." I sort of acknowledged this
insight politely and went on, but after a few more moments Joye
brought it up again: "There are no mothers in this play! I'm stuck in
this mother thing now." And I began to get it that in a group that is
mostly women, many of them mothers and grandmothers, this is naturally important. In addition it's a deep insight into Shakespeare's craft,
and one I had never encountered before; he wants a cold world with
savagely competitive sisters, so he robs them of a mother who might
have mediated. Again, this seeming digression becomes part of the play
with Yvette first asking, "Don't these girls have a mother?" and when
told, "No, there are no mothers in this play," responding, "No mothers!
No wonder it's a tragedy!" Later, after Cordelia is exiled, she adds, "If
there was a mother here, this would never have happened."

The protestations of love by Goneril and Regan,

Sir,
I love you more than word can wield the matter
Dearer than eyesight, space and liberty

73

first provoke outrage at their hypocrisy, but eventually recognition, that while we may not be as brazen—or as skilled—as they are, we all flatter those in power—parents, grandchildren, bosses, teachers. Further, we acknowledge how we use love, real or feigned, to get what we need and demand love in return for what we have to give. So, at this point, David steps in and suggests a flattery circle in which we all just say flattering words, phrases or sentences:

You look great!
Love your shoes.
What a mind!
Did you lose weight?
Didn't I just see you in something?
Great haircut!
Can I have your autograph?
I would never tell anyone else, but I know I can trust you.
Mom, you're the greatest!
That must have cost a mint!

We come out of it, dripping with disgust at our own hypocrisy, more forgiving of Goneril and Regan, and angry at Lear.

We go back to the text:

LEAR: And now, our joy, our youngest, Cordelia,
    Although our last and least, what can you say to draw
    A third more opulent than your sisters?
CORDELIA: Nothing, my lord.
LEAR: Nothing?
CORDELIA: Nothing.

And so on until Yvette bursts in:

There is no compassion for an elderly parent in this scene, and none from Cordelia where you would expect.

Cindy responds,

She's teaching him a lesson. I also think it is her individuating from that kind of control.

And we're off!

74

Yvette says that when she was a young woman, like Cindy, she completely identified and sympathized with Cordelia, the truth teller, the rebel, who refuses to play along with Lear's horrible game. But now that she herself is closer to Lear's age, she sees it differently:

> Isn't there a little hubris in her refusing to say anything? There's a haughtiness there. She's not giving him what he needs. She's very self-righteous about this whole thing of not being hypocritical but also it may be that she doesn't love him. Would it hurt so much to tell him she loves him?

Muriel and Molly, both elders, defend Cordelia:

MURIEL: She just can't do more than she's saying. "Obey you, love you, and most honor you."

MOLLY: This is what parents expect from children—obey, honor, love them. That's ordinary. Cordelia is saying, "What you want from me, you have from me. You just happen to be really mistaken."

The discussion goes on, divided not young against old, but those who are, at least in theory, for truth at whatever cost, versus those who accept some lies for the sake of peace.

Text reading and study, discussion and storytelling go on for two full workshops. Finally, we read the scene straight through one more time. It is full of fire and conflict—and pleasure at how far we have come. Even Muriel agrees that, while Shakespeare is very hard work, he is worth it.

The fourth workshop begins with: Each actor makes a statement accompanied by a gesture and the whole group repeats the statement and the gesture.

This time the question is: If your kids would have to compete to get the biggest part of your legacy, what would they have to do?

> The child who calls me everyday twice a day and that's it.
> The child who moves back to New York City.
> The one who sends me on the best vacation.
> The one who brings me a movie every night and watches it with me.
> The child who cooks me the best, most nutritious food.

The one who keeps the garden weeded.
The one who makes me smile when I'm down.
The one who laughs at all my jokes.
The child who minds its own business.
The kid who produces a grandchild for us.
The one who brushes my hair and makes tea.
The one who doesn't remember every story I told and lets me tell
    it again.
The child who gives me unconditional love.

Then we sit and ask: Pick a line from the play that you could imagine using in a situation in your own life. Tell a little anecdote with the line included.

I had a crush on this guy. I gave him my number. What should I do? I already left a message, I left two messages. "Love and be silent."

A lawyer friend told us that we should ask the kids what they want in the house, "that future strife may be prevented now." Well, it totally flopped. They said, "We don't want to talk about that, it's ridiculous."

I helped deliver my first grandchild and it was a long, hard delivery and finally the baby came out. My son was holding the baby and I really felt, "I love you more than word can wield the matter; Dearer than eyesight, space, and liberty." No feeling for a man or anything else can compare to seeing your eternity going on.

The scene is really getting under our skins now, and we're ready for the next exercise:

The actors are paired off, young/old. First, each tells the other a story evoked by the scene from your own life or that you have heard. Then, together make a presentation of the two stories, either in separate vignettes, or synthesize the two stories into one. Subjects can, for example, be legacies, sibling rivalry, the elder giving up the caretaking to a younger person, or any opinions about behavior that are evoked.

Also, choose a line from the Shakespeare scene that relates to your story, and use it either as the title or place it at the climactic moment in your scene. The story doesn't have to be a direct illustration of that line.

The resulting four-minute vignette can take the form of storytelling or a combination of storytelling and dramatization.

Here are two vignettes, slightly edited for length. In the first, twenty-year-old Annie plays her own father, and Esther, a Root, plays Annie's sister (they kept those roles in the production as well).

ESTHER: Dad. Dad, I have to speak to you.

ANNIE: Yeah. Yeah, what's on your mind? Problem there with your boss?

ESTHER: No, No. Everything is fine.

ANNIE: Financially, you're . . .

ESTHER: Set. I'm making buckets of money. It's kind of a social problem, Dad. I don't know how to start . . .

ANNIE: Are you starting to date a little bit more?

ESTHER: Well . . .

ANNIE: Dating some other guys?

ESTHER: I tried for a while but no, it's Sean. I'm really serious about him.

ANNIE: You know, Julie, your mother and I feel that you're better than him. And I don't want you hanging around with him and his loser friends. He's not going anywhere. You're a smart girl, you are my daughter.

ESTHER: But you don't know him.

ANNIE: Neither do you. I know enough, more about that kid than I ever wanted to know. And I can't believe that my daughter is dating him.

ESTHER: But you don't know him the way I know him, Dad.

ANNIE: How often is he at your new apartment? I mean, Julie, you know, we're both adults here.

ESTHER: As much as possible, Dad. That's the truth.

ANNIE: All right, you know what, I don't know that I even want to talk about this anymore frankly. You know how your mother and I feel. And if you want to go against us and go down that road, that's fine. It makes me sick, though.

ESTHER: Dad, It's not that simple. I'm carrying his child.

Silence.

Did you hear me, Dad? I'm pregnant.

ANNIE: How can you walk into this house and tell me that you're pregnant with his child?!

ESTHER: Because I love you, Dad.

ANNIE: Oh, forget about that—you don't love me! You are mixed up. Are you going to have this baby?

ESTHER: I don't know. (*Pause*) Yes, I will.

ANNIE: All right. Well, you know what, let me tell you something. You have defied your mother and you have defied me. Unless you turn your back on that piece of shit, and you come back to this house and let me, your mother, your sisters and aunts and uncles help you. We will support you financially, we will give that baby the love he deserves, and your mother will take care of that baby when you're at work—if you say no to a life of things that I don't even want to talk about. What do you have to say?

ESTHER: Nothing.

ANNIE: Nothing?

ESTHER: Nothing.

ANNIE: Then, I here disclaim all my paternal care, propinquity, and property of blood, and as a stranger to my heart and me hold thee from this forever, my former daughter.

This was a stunning moment; *King Lear* come to life in our midst. There was much questioning of Annie, which revealed that since the baby was born, there had been a reconciliation. In fact, just as the father in the scene offers, the baby stays with his grandparents every day while the mother works. Almost every scene is followed by an interlude of spontaneous and group-generated discussion. There is never any need for formal "deroling" or "decompression."

In the second, Sabine plays her own father, and Yvette plays Sabine.

Telephone rings.

SABINE: Hello.

FATHER: How are you doing, "our joy, although our last and least?"

SABINE: Hi, Dad! Oh, I'm fine. How are you and Mom? Are you exhausted from the wedding?

FATHER: Oh, yeah, yeah. It's nice being home, I guess. How's . . . How's New York?

SABINE: New York is fine, but I have to tell you again and again what a fantastic wedding you made for my sister. It was done with such style and elegance and love. And everybody had a good time and she enjoyed it and her husband felt so welcomed into the family. I want to thank you for doing it that way.

FATHER: You know weddings—emotional.

SABINE: Oh, sure.

FATHER: But your sister's really happy now.

SABINE: She is, Dad.

FATHER: She . . . she did well. I couldn't have given her away to a better guy. I really couldn't have.

SABINE: Good. And I hope when the time comes, I hope you and my future husband will have a good relationship—

FATHER: Well, you still have a lot of time. You do your theater thing and you still have so much time.

SABINE: Oh, yeah. But young people think about these things.

FATHER: So how is New York?

SABINE: New York is fine.

FATHER: You're learning a lot?

SABINE: I'm learning a lot!

FATHER: And you're studying a lot?

SABINE: And I'm loving it.

FATHER: That's good.

SABINE: Dad, are you all right?

FATHER: You know what, honey, I sort of have to go now.

SABINE: No, no, no, no.

FATHER: I'll give you a call on Sunday.

SABINE: No, don't you dare hang up!

FATHER: I really have to go. We have all these workers coming—

SABINE: I don't care. I don't like that tone of voice.

FATHER: I'll call you on Sunday, okay?

SABINE: No, that's not okay. That's three days off, and I don't like your tone of voice and there's something wrong. Are you and Mom okay?

FATHER: Your mother's fine! Your mother's always fine!

SABINE: What about you?

FATHER: I'm fine.

SABINE: You're upsetting me too much. I'm sorry, Dad. I can't wait until Sunday for you to tell me? Hello?

FATHER: Just don't forget me. Don't forget me.

Most of the other vignettes were equally stunning, and I wish there were room here to reproduce them all. But these two, with minimal editing, fit right into the play, woven into the Division scene. At the time, however, we had no idea, nor were we even thinking about, how any of this might fit into a Roots&Branches production of *King Lear*. We were just trying to explore the text in our own way, with the trust that somehow, sometime in the future we would make a play from all that happened along the way.

The Thank-You Circle

Most workshops end with a *thank-you circle*. We stand in a circle, and each actor thanks someone else for something they said or did during the workshop that really struck them. The pattern is to say, "Thank you, (name), for . . ." and then perform that moment. For example, "Thank you for . . .

Shakespeare makes me stand up straight and think fast.

I would like to pass on—certainly to my grandchildren, my children if it's not too late—a sense of commitment and passion to people and things of the world.

How did my Aunt Rosie's nose get on my face?

Just tell me if it's still all blue there.

You should get the Madonna and Child, not the Renoir!

I'm not crawling to my grave.

There are no mothers in this play!

No feeling for a man or anything else can compare to seeing your eternity going on.

Just don't forget me. Don't forget me.

The thank-you circle serves not only to complete the workshop, but also as a quick review of the day's work. It's important to know what sticks with people, as we will see when we get to creating the script. In addition, the thank-you circle recognizes the contributions everyone makes to the process. It is not a rule, no one articulated the need to acknowledge everyone, it just quietly became part of our practice to make sure everyone is thanked in the form of celebrating something they did during the workshop.

In four workshops, one month, we went from a group of rather timid strangers in the strange land of Shakespeare and *King Lear*, to intimate familiarity with the major characters, a deep sense of connection between our lives and feelings and those remote kings and princesses, and a sense that we could master this monster. We had told ourselves the story, read and studied the text closely, discussed it vigorously and at length, improvised off it, and developed a process for working with the rest of the text. In a variety of ways, we had also discovered how our own lives reveal and are revealed by the towering world of Shakespeare. As a friend said after seeing the production, *Playing Lear*, "Your stories make the Shakespeare accessible, and the Shakespeare elevates your personal stories."[12]

Life Stories, Discussion, Improvisation, and Text

Each season, with each new project, we have to reinvent these elements. This year we are working with fairy tales, so, compared to *King Lear*, the text work is simple—everyone knows the stories or can read them with ease. The real discovery is how these iconic stories and characters affect our lives, both empowering us and blocking our journey toward maturity and wholeness. So we are looking for improvisations and story themes that will expose in each of us the princess, prince, ogre, witch, dumb son, evil stepmother, and so on. In addition, we have to find a presentational form in a way that we didn't with *King Lear*, where the basic structure of the play was a given, and the challenge was to find how to work with it.

The goal in this section has been to describe a particular set of workshops in as much messy detail as possible in the hope that it gives you a sense of the spirit of play and exploration that informs our work. Obviously, we have no paradigm, but there is an underlying structure, a narrative, based on careful attention to who and what we are and where we are going.

4

Creating a Script

Excerpt from *The Subway Series* (1999)

This scene occurs about a third of the way into The Subway Series. *The play takes place on a subway in New York. The train is stalled for the usual impenetrable reasons, and after young and old take their frustration out on each other, the Conductor announces that their negativity is draining energy from the third rail, and until their conflicts are worked out, the train will be traveling through time, running on the A for Ageism line. They travel back through the decades and arrive at this stop.*

CONDUCTOR: All right! Enough Cold War. Let's go back to some real stuff. You kids need to know what shaped these people. So we're going to go back to the time when they were the same age as you kids are now. Next stop, 1942.
YVETTE: 1942!
CONDUCTOR: Station stop is 1942. Exit here for World War II.
MADAME ZEITGEIST: (*A gypsy fortune-teller-type character, except she tells the present. With her arm around Yvette, who peers out from the car as if looking at the world of 1942*) Can you see it? A nation totally mobilized, a president we idolized, big bands and black outs, Joe DiMaggio, rationing, segregation, hats, gloves, nylons, garter belts, and union busting. Expressions like "hubba hubba," "victory gardens," . . .
YVETTE: And "Send a salami to your boy in the army."
CONDUCTOR: And, "Stop driving and ride the subway," because, "He who drives alone, drives with Hitler!"

Three women on the subway make like the Andrews Sisters singing "Don't sit under the apple tree with anyone else but me."

YVETTE: 1942! I got married that year. I was . . .

YOUNG YVETTE: (*Dressed 1940s style, turns on bench to face audience as young Yvette*) I am . . .

BOTH: (*They both touch their hair the same way*) Seventeen years old.

ARIEL: Seventeen! I'm already twenty and I can't imagine getting married. At seventeen I was a total baby.

YVETTE: So was I. But it was such a different time. The war was on. The boys were joining the army.

Men in military caps stand upstage as straphangers. They hold straps as if hanging from the ceiling of the car.

And going off to fight, and the girls were all showing off their engagement rings.

Women gather as straphangers with men and show off rings.

And I met this handsome boy,

Soldier enters in military uniform, sits at DC of car facing audience next to Young Yvette.

And he looked so good in his uniform, and. . . .

SOLDIER: Gee, this is swell.

YOUNG YVETTE: I'm having a great time.

SOLDIER: Look, we're above ground, you can see the Statue of Liberty out there.

YOUNG YVETTE: Wow, she's beautiful! I loved Coney Island. I would never have gone on the tilt-a-whirl if it weren't for you.

SOLDIER: The whole world is a tilt-a-whirl these days.

YOUNG YVETTE: I'll say.

SOLDIER: You know, I can hardly believe this is only our second date. Where have you been all my life?

YOUNG YVETTE: (*Blushes*)

Pause, they look out at the river.

SOLDIER: Well I'm shipping out next week.

YOUNG YVETTE: Next week? Where to?

SOLDIER: They said I can't tell anyone.

YOUNG YVETTE: Of course; "Loose lips sink ships." I'm so proud of you. I wish I could fight right along with you guys.

SOLDIER: I hate those fascist bastards!

YOUNG YVETTE: Me too! (*Pause*) I'll miss you.

SOLDIER: Yeah, I'll miss you too. It's funny. . . . We hardly know each other.

They freeze while the straphangers behind them turn and speak over their shoulders toward the young couple.

CHORUS 1: Marry her. A guy needs a wife when he's going off to war.

CHORUS 2: Marry him, you'll have someone to wait for!

CHORUS 3: Unite the United States!

ALL: It's your patriotic duty.

The chorus freezes, couple resumes.

SOLDIER: You know we haven't known each other long, but I really like you.

YOUNG YVETTE: I like you too. I wish we had time to get to know each other better.

SOLDIER: Well, we don't have much time. I'll be gone in a week and who knows when I'll be back.

YOUNG YVETTE: A week?

SOLDIER: Yeah, look I wish we had two years to court and get to know each other, and meet the folks, but Der Fuhrer isn't giving us that luxury. We have to carpe diem, seize the day, gather ye rosebuds while we may.

YOUNG YVETTE: Yeah! . . . What do you mean?

SOLDIER: Let's spend every moment we've got together, what do you say. Night and day.

YOUNG YVETTE: Day and . . . night?

SOLDIER: Yeah my aunt is out of town and she gave me her apartment. We could have it all to ourselves.

Straphanger chorus as before.

CHORUS 1: Grab him while you can.

CHORUS 2: Do it now or the good ones will be gone.

CHORUS 3: See all those gold stars in the windows.

All: (*Echo*) in the windows . . . in the windows . . .

Chorus 4: Anyway, you want to get out of your parents' house. You want to have, you know . . .

ALL: (*Echo*) Sex . . . sex . . . sex.

YOUNG YVETTE: But we're not married.

SOLDIER: Baby there's a war on.

YOUNG YVETTE: But only the wild poets and Bolsheviks live together and have free love.

SOLDIER: Why in this insane world do we need a piece of paper?

YOUNG YVETTE: Because it makes it legal, and moral, and you don't get yelled at by your mother.

SOLDIER: Hey, you know, you're right. If we're fighting the fascists we have to stand up for what's right and moral and the rule of law and all that. I'll feel better going off to fight those bastards if I'm fighting for you, for us. . . . I'm not too good at this and I didn't have time to plan it or even buy you a ring, but . . .

YOUNG YVETTE: Ahem!

SOLDIER: Oh (*gets down on one knee*) Look, I know this is sudden and we don't know each other for a long time, but I really love you, kid, and I want to marry you and if I get back from this damn war we'll have a family and we'll be great together. What do you say?

ARIEL: (*Has been watching SR, across from Yvette*) Wait a minute! Patriotism? That's a reason to marry someone?

YVETTE: Maybe it's not now, but then every choice I made was affected by the war. I mean I couldn't throw away garbage without making sure I saved the rubber and tin foil. So something as important as marriage was very political.

ARIEL: And you were only seventeen?

JESS T: Now the pressure is to get a career, and if anyone I knew was getting married they'd say "What is your problem?" I'm sorry, it's like, sad.

ARIEL: Like they are throwing away their lives.

JESS T: Yeah and its horrible, at twenty-two to have kids. Your life is over; forget it.

ARIEL & JESS T: (*Join Joye and Marcy*)
And that song would go like:

Joye, Marcy, Ariel and Jess T don identical red-checked scarves and move like the Andrews Sisters, singing in close harmony, to the tune of "Don't Sit Under the Apple Tree."

Don't get tied in that marriage knot
knot not all that it seems
A bunch of romantic dreams
That burst out at the seams
No no no
Don't let some little urge you got
Get carried to such extremes
You'll end up stuck at home

And, Don't settle down till you explore
Your personality
Your possibility
Your sexuality
No no no
Keep on pushing that envelope
Toward your totality
You need more time to roam

And, Don't go getting down on your knee
Till I finish my MD
Make partner or VP
Or possibly all three
No no no
I'm not getting myself tied down
To those hormones and chemistry
I'd rather live alone

And, Don't go singin' that baby jive
It really isn't fair
Without a nanny or au pair
I'd pull out every hair
No no no
You stay home and change the diapers
And take her to day care
While I work my cell phone.

They finish with a flourish toward Yvette.

YVETTE: Well of course I would agree with you now. But then the voices in my head were saying . . .

Straphangers.

CHORUS 1: Marry him, and all the other girls will be jealous.
CHORUS 2: And you'll get his GI allowance. You could go to school and not have to work.
CHORUS 3: If you can imagine yourself washing his underwear, marry him!
ALL: It's your patriotic duty!
YVETTE: So I said, . . .
ANDREWS SISTERS: (*Singing in horror toward Young Yvette*) No, no, no!
YOUNG YVETTE: Yes, yes, . . .
BOTH YVETTES: Yes!

Young couple kiss like the famous WWII photo.

YVETTE: We got married three days later, and four days after that he shipped out for Europe (*Soldier marches DR, Young Yvette and Yvette wave, he tosses a jaunty farewell salute*)
I didn't see him for four years.

Chorus hums "As Time Goes By."

He signed all his letters,
SOLDIER: Death to the fascists! Love, your husband.
ARIEL: Not even his name?
YVETTE: No.
ARIEL: It's like it was more the role than the person.
YVETTE: I see that now, but then I thought it was adorable.

She puts her arm around Young Yvette and together they fade UL, Soldier UR.[13]

In Roots&Branches we tape-record every workshop and have them transcribed. The value of transcription, as opposed to taking notes, can't be exaggerated. Getting the exact wording can make all the difference. In the scene just read, Jess says, "I'm sorry, it's like, sad." If I were only taking notes, I might have missed that little gem of youth locution circa 1999, and certainly could never have made it up. And again, in our play *Old AIDS*, Minna said, "I did it once already for your mother." That is a word order and use of the word *already* that are unique to a time and place, and again, I could never make that up.

Okay, so now, after months of workshops, you have a stack of transcripts several inches high, enough for several plays. So how do you select what to use and what to let go? And then how do you weave all of that into an entertaining, provocative show, about one hour long, with good and appropriate material for each of your actors? It's a tall order, but manageable if you take it in small steps. Here's how we've come to do it.

Most playwriting teachers will emphasize the priority of structure and the well-made script. And that is a worthy goal, but for several reasons it can't be our first priority:

- The way we work: improvising and storytelling over months, doesn't lend itself to tight plots, character trajectories, and the elements of the well-made play.
- We need to provide challenging, appropriate material for each member of the ensemble.
- We have a very limited time in which to put the play together.

This doesn't mean that our plays aren't good provocative theater. Lots of wonderful productions are not *well-made* plays: from the works of experimental directors like Joseph Chaikin, Robert Wilson, Anne Bogart, and Richard Foreman, to cabaret, to the works of Caryl Churchill or Tony Kushner. They all have different agendas, which we accept if the work is strong, and so do we.

At this point—after many workshops and with a pile of transcript in hand—we need only a speculative sense of the structure or style of the play. Everything depends on the content. Our priority is choosing the best material from the workshops, then building a play around it.

So my collaborator, David Schechter, and I sit down in our favorite cafe of the moment, eat a good meal, then lean back and reminisce about the workshops. We compare notes on our favorite stories, improvs, and discussions. Nothing more, really, because at this point all we want to know is what struck one or both of us strongly enough to remember it weeks or months later. Neither of us has yet looked at the transcripts. Our first priority is what we remember, on the theory that if it made enough impact for us to recall it, there must be theatrical potential there. Clearly that is a risky proposition and subject to revision as we develop the script, but it is the best starting place.

Having collected the workshop moments we remembered best, with no sense of how they might fit together into a play, we then go to the transcripts, pull those "scenes" and only then start to read through. After a couple of sweeps we have more than enough to make a play. And, generally, our first thoughts, the stuff we remember, hold up quite well.

The fact is that you don't need a whole lot to put together an hour-long show; a beginning, three to five scenes, and an end should do it. It is at this point, when we have decided upon our material, that we then begin to think seriously about how to order it, and how to weave it together into a show. But still, the priority is on creating good scenes, and allowing the structure—style, form, sequence, segues, and so on—to flow from them.

Because there are a lot of actors on stage, and you want to give everyone something to do, it is tempting to write various kinds of sequences of short lines, divided equally among the actors. Be afraid; be very afraid! This sort of dialogue depends so much on rhythm and timing that it demands great skill from the actors. Skilled and unskilled actors of all ages have trouble with it. Add on to that memory issues, along with hearing and sight problems, and you have the makings of disaster. It can work if you keep it fairly short, substantive, and you have time to drill it over and over, including before every show. But we have had many more disasters than successes with this.

Working on Chekhov's *Three Sisters*, we became enamored of the question, "What is your Moscow?" Just as the sisters long to go to Moscow, where they dream that their lives would be transformed and fulfilled, we all have daydreams and unattainable longings. The group came up with a wonderful list, and I put it in the script, carefully edited for rhythm and poetry. It sounded great on paper and sometimes in rehearsal, but in almost every performance someone forgot to come in or came in at the wrong place, and that would throw the whole thing off, so it never really worked. So, how do we go about making scenes from transcript?

Creating a Scene

In this section we'll follow the development of the scene that opens this chapter. It evolved from a simple story told in a workshop and went through many false starts and revisions before it reached its final form. The problem is how to take a story told in an intimate setting into theater that can communicate to large numbers of strangers.

Scenes evolve in all kinds of ways. This is only one example. There is no formula for this work, it always varies, but I hope that from this example you will derive inspiration and a sense of how, through a lot of trial and error, we arrive at our plays.

First go back and read the finished scene again, and then read the section to see how it evolved.

The Story

This is one of those stories I never forgot. Early in the fall of 1999, we began focusing on the theme of "then and now." We started with contrasts of styles and customs, but quickly moved on to an interest in how ways of thinking and experiencing the world change over time. We explored this terrain from a number of approaches. One was a homework assignment: to think of a story from your life that could only have happened the way it did at a particular moment in history. In other words, the politics, zeitgeist, culture, and whatever else of the time had a significant effect on the way the story turned out.

Here is the unedited transcription of one of the stories told in response to our assignment.

> There's one particular time in my life that could only have happened at the time that it did, and that was my getting married (in 1942). Because I was seventeen, and you had to support the war effort. One way to support it was by giving a guy in the army a reason to fight the fascists. For years my husband would end his love letters, "Death to the Fascists! Love, your husband." It was a united United States—the last war everyone was gung-ho for. And partly it was I wanted to give this particular guy someone to think about and write to while he was overseas, and someone to come home to. But part of it was the guys were leaving, there was a decimation of the male population, and girls

were getting desperate at sixteen and seventeen. If we didn't get married then we might never have another chance because all the guys who were still alive would get grabbed up and the other guys were dead. So there was less of a chance, hopefully than now. But it was very much a political milieu, and the atmosphere was about patriotic duty.

Discussion

Stories provoke stories in response—as Barbara Myerhoff said, "A story isn't a story until it receives a story in return."[14] And a strong story like this one will provoke a lot of storytelling and discussion. As with all discussions, it wandered widely—to other wars (Korea, Vietnam), the Atomic Bomb, postwar marriage, divorce, when did the word *relationship* come to be used in the context of love, and so on. These *digressions* are invaluable, because often they also become grist for the play, or at least for future improvs, so don't discourage digression. But, for the purposes of this chapter, we have cut a lot from the transcript and focused on the parts that became grist for this particular scene.

The Roots are Yvette, Selma, Sam, Esther, Michaela, and Marcy. The Branches are Joye, Dera, Jessica, Erica, Nick, and Ariel.

SELMA: My friends that were not much older than me were getting married, so I got married, what the hell, it was true.

SAM: A girl was considered twenty-four or twenty-five—things were looking bad.

ESTHER: At twenty-one you were an old maid. A guy you were dating casually you might never see again, suddenly he was the most important thing in your life. I remember it was with great difficulty that I went anywhere near Grand Central or Penn station because all of that meant good-bye. I happened to get engaged just before Pearl Harbor in 1941 and was caught up in the drama.

YVETTE: And you knew people who died, all the guys you went to high school with. You would see a black flag with a gold star on the door, or in the window. So it was all very personal, you didn't read about it you saw it.

JOYE: Did you feel pressured by him to marry him?

YVETTE: Not any more pressure than what I put on myself.

SELMA: Did you have a child right away?

YVETTE: Fortunately no, he was overseas for a few years, and our first child was born four years after we were married.

SELMA: My husband never saw me pregnant with my first child and came home when she was six months old. It was rough. It was really rough.

DERA: I'm angry.

SELMA: How could you be angry, what would make you angry?

DERA: Well it's just different now because now you have a choice to go to war.

YVETTE: But this was a war you believed in you wanted to go. You had no personal life; absolutely everything was tied up in the war. . . . It was in our life for a very long time.

DERA: The boys that I know don't have the same patriotism that they did then, no matter the cause, they have nothing to prove as males, they don't feel it is their duty.

SELMA: The thinking changed with the Vietnam War. (*Echoes of* yes) When my son left he was waving flags with his toes, and he volunteered. And when he got there he wrote, "Get me the fuck home." He wrote it just like that, "Get me the fuck home."

DIRECTOR: I'm wondering about the pressure to get married. Do any of the younger people feel that pressure to get married ever, or what is the pressure now?

JESSICA: Now the pressure is to get a career, and if anyone I knew was getting married we'd say what is their problem? I'm sorry, it's like sad.

ARIEL: Like they are throwing away their lives.

JESSICA: Yeah and it's horrible, at twenty-two to have kids. Your life is over, forget it.

JOYE: I feel that changes when you get to your later twenties. (*Echoes of* yes) I mean I'm twenty-seven—almost twenty-eight, and I've started thinking, and it's strange for me, 'cause I do have a lot of friends married or getting married and babies. And now my grandmother is going, "So, what, you're going to have a career? Is this going to be your thing?" And I feel like I'm at the baby end of getting that pressure at twenty-eight. And that's a major change between the generations.

DERA: My parents don't want me in a relationship, because they think it will take away from my studies. Especially now with marriage not even happening until you're thirty.

ERICA: I feel like the pressure to get married for me is more cultural. (*Erica is Chicana, from SW Texas, a very different background from most of the group, who are white and urban*) Because ever since I was little I can remember dreaming about getting married. But my mother said, "Not 'til you get your masters degree!" And what she always wanted for her daughters was for them to be able to support themselves without a man. My mom was the oldest to get married at twenty-five, she was the only one to graduate from college, and her sisters were getting married at sixteen. And my cousins, we've always been very close the three of us, one is married, and one is practically engaged. So I feel the pressure. But I think at the same time I know I'm nowhere near financially emotionally ready for that. I want to have my shit together before I bring anyone else in. (*Applause*)

SELMA: You wanted to have sex so you got married. You couldn't live together first.

YVETTE: Right!

JESSICA: I will never marry someone before I live with them.

JOYE: But it's a bad idea. Because everyone starts pressuring you about marriage; they realize the economic benefits; they just decide, "what the hell," and it doesn't come from them or their passion.

NICK: It's all very scary. I have no interest in anything happening like that for a long long time. But I just heard this term, DINK— "Double Income No Kids." And that sounds pretty good to me.

ESTHER: Only the wild poets and Bolsheviks lived together and had free love.

Improvs

Yvette's story and the ensuing discussion touched on many facets of our theme—the uniqueness of the time, the connections between personal lives and history, cultural pressures in the air, social mores, and the enormous gap between people's attitudes then and now toward when and

93

why to marry. In order to explore this further, we set up an improv. We wondered how a marriage proposal in 1942 might compare to one today. So we set up two simultaneous improvs, one taking place in 1942, the other in the present. In each, a young couple discusses getting married. Two elders, who were there, played the 1942 couple, and two young people played the present day couple. (Obviously, for other kinds of takes or ends, the ages could be switched around.) To add spice, we adapted a common improv technique and included "consultants," young and old. The lovers could turn out of the scene for "consultations," and the consultants could interrupt to give advice or ask questions. The director called out when to change from one era to the other.

Again, the raw transcript has been shortened, but not otherwise revised.

Courtship 1942 and 1999

1942

YVETTE: Well ya know if you go overseas, and all the guys are getting shipped out, and I don't want you to get killed, would you like someone back home as a wife to come home to, and send your GI allowance to? I could go to school and not have to work.

RICHARD: This is sort of one-sided. You're telling me I might get killed and you get the insurance.

YVETTE: Yeah I'd get that too.

RICHARD: You know I come from a very large family, and marriage is a great institution.

CONSULTANT: (*To Richard*) Is this the woman you want to spend your whole life with?

RICHARD: (*Aside to consultant*) Well I have to decide that now. Give me a chance.

CONSULTANT: Be careful don't rush in.

YVETTE: Where were you?

RICHARD: (*Comes back*) Well I'm here on 30-day leave and we could go and . . .

YVETTE: Not unless we're married.

RICHARD: What?

YVETTE: I know what you're going to say.

RICHARD: What do you mean you know?

YVETTE: I know.

RICHARD: What I was going to say is that my aunt went down to Florida and we. . . .

CONSULTANT: (*To Yvette*) Consultation! So what if we did sleep with him?

YVETTE: (*Aside*) Without being married?

CONSULTANT: Why do you need marriage?

YVETTE: Well, because it makes it legal, and moral, and you don't get yelled at by your mother.

DIRECTOR: Switch!

1999

NICK: Joye, we've been living together for three years now, I think it's time . . .

JOYE: To break up?

CONSULTANT: (*to Joye*) Consultation! Remember you have a joint banking account.

JOYE: So you were saying . . .

NICK: I've been getting a lot of pressure from a lot of people, and I think I'm ready, I think we're ready to—

JOYE: to . . . to . . . to?

NICK: (*Aside*) Consultation—what am I doing? I don't want to get married.

CONSULTANT: Change the subject; do anything.

NICK: Did you see 20/20 last night?

JOYE: No I didn't, was it about marriage? Is that how—who put this in your head?

NICK: Let's get married.

JOYE: Why now?

NICK: Why not now?

CONSULTANT: (*To Joye*) Consultation. You got a larger problem here, he's got another apartment uptown that's much nicer, I think you ought to consider that offer. Also he's got some money.

JOYE: Yeah, his family is wealthy.

CONSULTANT: What about your job, what about your career, what about your friends, what about your life, what are you going to do?

JOYE: (*To Nick*) Will this affect my job, career, life, or friends?

NICK: Of course not.

JOYE: Honey I don't know, honey look, I think that, we've had three years.

NICK: Yeah I know and we're practically married so I think that we should—

JOYE: You know we are practically married so what's the difference, what's the point? My parents love you. Your parents love me, we all get along, and that piece of paper is just going to ruin it. Ruins it for everyone, look what happened to Mark and Alice—they

NICK: Well Mark and Alice . . .

CONSULTANT: So what do you feel about him?

JOYE: Well I love him.

CONSULTANT: Are you sure?

JOYE: Yes! (*To Nick*) Well I know that I love you.

NICK: And I know that I love you too— Consultation. So why is it so important for this piece of paper?

CONSULTANT: She doesn't seem like she's into it. I mean what do you think.

NICK: I think I love this girl. I think it's a nice old-fashioned thing to do, get married and ahh and just make it legal.

JOYE: So what's the deal? Do you want kids?

NICK: No absolutely not, you've got your career I've got mine . . .

JOYE: You don't want kids?

NICK: No I'd love to have kids eventually.

JOYE: Eventually, well how long? How many kids do you want to have?

NICK: How many? Do you know how much private school costs these days?

DIRECTOR: Switch!

1942

RICHARD: So as I was saying I just need to have a little trial. I'm not signing anything. I could get killed. This could be the last days of my life.

YVETTE: I know.

RICHARD: I thought we could live together.

YVETTE: Not as if we were married. It's not right.

RICHARD: Why?

YVETTE: Because.

RICHARD: You mean to tell me all this lovey dovey . . .

YVETTE: I love you very much but a girl can't be too careful—got to get married before you . . .

RICHARD: Well, we could dry hump.

CONSULTANT: Consul-f'ing-tation! Let's just look at him and picture him say forty-five years from now, I mean just look at him.

YVETTE: Very smart, good sense of humor.

CONSULTANT: But by that time he'll be senile.

YVETTE: No we're together and laughing.

CONSULTANT: If you're sure. I just want you to know I'm nervous.

YVETTE: Well so am I and I think he is too. (*To Richard*) Are you nervous, honey, about how this is going to work out?

RICHARD: I'm nervous in 'da service.

DIRECTOR: Switch!

1999

JOYE: I really am sorry, I don't want to throw you off about how I feel about you but I'm just really nervous about all this but I think we work really well as we are.

NICK: Yeah we do really work, so just take your time and think about it.

JOYE: Yes time, we have all the time in the world.

CONSULTANT: Consultation.

JOYE: Whaaaaat!?

CONSULTANT: I want you to be careful how you handle this. He's a good catch. Hold on to the rope with the other hand.

JOYE: Nick, I don't want you to think I will take too long with this— I'm just going to think about it for bit.

NICK: Let's just have an open dialogue.

JOYE: Maybe we could go to couples therapy.

NICK: Well the Bermans did that, and they left each other.

JOYE: They were married! That was the problem; they should have done that first.

Excerpts from the postimprov discussion

SELMA: I worried about laundry, I figured: If I could wash his underwear I could love him.

MARCY: I just couldn't believe that after you were married you
   needed to know how to do everything—cook, clean . . .
JOYE: We do all that now. Even when you're a kid. I did those things;
   Mom's not home to do them. She's working.

Conceptualizing a Scene

All through the fall, while the stories, improvs and discussions were
going on and being transcribed, the director, creative consultant, and
the group looked for a theatrical structure that would best frame the
scenes and bring out the themes. Many possibilities came up: a mys-
tery or sci-fi fantasy involving time travel; even a quilt that told stories. Always there was the question of finding a setting and a frame
where young and old might plausibly be together. Finally, inspired, as
I recall, by daily travel plus telling the story of *The Phantom Tollbooth*
to a child, the idea emerged of a subway car that travels through time,
and a conductor who wants to teach the riders to understand and care
for each other.

Again it can't be emphasized enough that the first priority is presenting the strongest material from the workshops. The structure, the
overall story, and the setting are devices to frame that material.

After some trial and error, we realized that within the time-
traveling subway frame, the conductor could take the younger people
back to 1942 to show them why it might have made sense to marry at
seventeen then, even though it makes no sense to them now. We did-
n't yet know where the young couple would be in relation to the subway—on it, or outside it, being watched from inside. Nor did we know
if Yvette should play herself in 1942, age seventeen, or should a young
woman play her? The answers, which seem obvious now, weren't then.
So, using some material from the improvs and discussions, and some
invented dialogue, we sketched out a scene. We tried it with old and
young couples, which made it clear that it would be stronger in this
case to have the young couple played by young people.

With that decision made, we saw that Yvette could both introduce
or segue into the scene, and stand beside it, watching her young self
making this momentous decision. And on the other side, physically
framing the scene, would be the young women who couldn't believe

anyone as smart as Yvette could have been "dumb" enough to marry at so young an age.

The initial draft of the scene had elements of the final, but it went through many tweakings. The group tried many versions with different casts, commenting as we went. Language was argued over and revised or cut based on comments from the ensemble. For example, the elders objected to the expression "Oh, you kid," which appears in the following draft, informing me that it came from a different time. So it went. And they objected to calling him "Herr Hitler." It was intended ironically, and to be said with contempt, but that still wasn't good enough. Finally they agreed that the young soldier would say, contemptuously, "Der Fuhrer." In addition there were numerous discussions about how young men and women would sit or stand or touch each other or dress in 1942. A young woman would wear gloves and a hat; she would sit much straighter than today; she would blush more easily; she would smile; she might disagree, but only by indirection; she would demand certain courtesies.

Another big problem was how to present the inner thoughts of the young couple, the voices of the historical moment, the zeitgeist. The character of Madame Zeitgeist, a sort of fortune-teller who tells the present, served to set the scene. But we also wanted to create a sense of the pressures on these lovers in the moment of decision. So we played with the idea of a chorus that could whisper in their ears, saying things like, "Marry him! It's your patriotic duty."

Draft Version

CONDUCTOR: This train is going local to 1942. (*Station sign says 1942*)

Intro music: swing band rendition of "Don't Sit Under the Apple Tree (With Anyone Else But Me)"; young couple dancing joyfully, digging the music, each other. He is in uniform, or enough parts—hat, jacket, and shiny shoes—to suggest a soldier/sailor in WWII. She has something 1940s on, too. Others emerge from subway, and put on hats or gloves and purse or apron, and so on to suggest the 1940s. Some dance in background, others stand in groupings. Music fades down and young couple comes Down Right arm in arm.

HE: Gee, this is swell.

SHE: I'm having a great time.

HE: Let's just sit and look at the river, what do you say?

SHE: Okay.

They sit on chairs or a bench. He tentatively puts his arm around her.

HE: You know, I can hardly believe this is only our second date. Where you been all my life?

SHE: Oh, you kid!

Pause, they look out at the river.

HE: Well I'm shipping out next week.

SHE: Where to?

HE: They said I can't tell anyone.

SHE: I'm so proud of you, I wish I could fight right along with you guys.

HE: I hate those fascist bastards.

SHE: Me too . . . I'll miss you.

HE: Yeah I'll miss you too. It's funny . . . we hardly know each other.

They freeze while behind them forms a chorus of men in army, navy hats, or homburgs and women of different ages wearing 1940s hats or gloves or aprons.

Ask her, then you'll have someone to think about and write to while you're overseas.

Marry him, then he'll have a reason to fight Hitler and Tojo.

You'll have someone to come home to.

You'll have someone to wait for.

Support the war effort. It's your patriotic duty.

Unite the United States!

The chorus freezes, couple resumes.

HE: You know, we haven't known each other long, but I really like you.

SHE: I like you too. I wish we had time to get to know each other better.

HE: Well, we don't have much time. I'll be gone in a week and who knows when I'll be back.

100

SHE: A week.

HE: Yeah, look I wish we had two years to court and get to know each other, and meet the folks, but Herr Hitler isn't giving us that luxury. We have to carpe diem, seize the day, gather ye rosebuds while we may.

SHE: Yeah! . . . What do you mean?

HE: Let's spend every moment we've got together, what do you say? Night and day.

SHE: Night and day?

HE: Yeah my aunt is out of town and she gave me her apartment. We could have it all to ourselves.

Chorus closes in on the couple and whispers.

Grab him while you can.

You might never see him again.

Do it now or the good ones will be gone.

They'll all be gone.

A lot of them aren't coming back.

See all those gold stars in the windows (*echo* in the windows, in the windows).

By the time this war is over, you'll be an old maid.

You want to get out of your parents' house. You want to have sex.

SHE: But we're not married.

HE: Baby there's a war on.

SHE: But only the wild poets and Bolsheviks live together and have free love.

HE: Why in this insane world do we need a piece of paper?

SHE: Because it makes it legal, and moral, and you don't get yelled at by your mother.

CHORUS: Ask her.

You might die next week.

She's a good kid, she's fun.

She's got a great body.

You'll have someone to write home to.

Someone to dream about besides Betty Grable.

HE: Hey, you know, you're right. If we're fighting the fascists we have to stand up for what's right and moral and the rule of law and all that. I'll feel better going off to fight those bastards if I'm fighting for you, for us. . . . I'm not too good at this and I didn't have time to plan it or even buy you a ring, but . . .

SHE: Ahem!

HE: Oh (*gets down on one knee*) look, I know this is sudden and we don't know each other for a long time, but I really love you, kid, and I want to marry you and if I get back from this damn war we'll have a family and we'll be great together. What do you say?

CHORUS:

If you don't marry him you might never see him again.

And you'll get his GI allowance. You could go to school and not have to work.

And if, God forbid, he gets killed, you'll get the insurance.

He's good-looking, smart, good sense of humor . . .

If you can imagine yourself washing his underwear, marry him!

(*All*) It's your patriotic duty!

SHE: Well, . . . why not?

YVETTE: We got married three days later and four days after that he shipped out for Europe. I didn't see him for four years. He signed all his letters, "Death to the fascists! Love, your husband." Not even his name. It was more the role than the person.

DERA: I'm angry.

YVETTE: How could you be angry? What would make you angry?

DERA: Well it's just different now.

YVETTE: Tell, tell . . .

CONDUCTOR: Step in! Watch the closing doors! This train is reversing direction and proceeding to the end of the century. Next stop 1972.

As train passes through decades, various emblems of the times appear, or Madame Zeitgeist announces the present.

CONDUCTOR: Station stop is 1972. Let them off, let 'em off.

Marcy gets on with headband and carrying a joint. Dera spots her, grabs her hand, and takes her over to the conductor.

DERA: (*To conductor*) Excuse me; I'm in a hurry to get on with my life. Can't we go express to the end of the line?

CONDUCTOR: Oh, well . . .

MARCY: (*Takes a toke and passes joint to conductor*) Eere!
CONDUCTOR: (*Takes it and*) Next stop, the present.

As you see, the chorus is sketchy, and the language rough, but the shape is there. It took a while to realize that the scene could take place *on* the subway, rather than outside it.

Once the context and form of the boy–girl scene were clear, we turned to the Chorus. How could they be both a natural and acceptable part of the scene and also speak the voices in the minds of the young lovers, pressuring them toward an early unexamined marriage? A lot of what they might say was already available from the improvisations, and further improvs purely on that theme produced more. These we call *guided improvisations*, and we use them often when the script is in development. Often it is only at this stage that we find that we need a particular scene or type of material, so rather than writing it entirely ourselves, David and I go back to the group and set up an improv designed to fill the gap. In this case the problem was more formal than substantive, but the group was just as instrumental in solving it.

We tried having the chorus members sit on the subway and then rise and speak into the young lovers' ears; we tried having the subway stop each time the chorus came in, walk by outside and whisper in the window. Then one day Sam mentioned the word *straphangers*, and it all came clear. (For those who don't know the term, in 1942 and for a long time after, the subways had leather straps hanging from horizontal bars, with wooden or plastic handles that could be held by standing riders. Thus the term *straphangers* came to be, which is still used as a nickname for subway riders, even though only the older ones would have any idea what it refers to.) Our designer, Tine Kindermann, made straps that stood up straight on their own, and the Chorus stood with their backs to the young lovers, holding their straps and jiggling as if the subway were running. They looked as if they were eavesdropping, and when the Chorus segments came, they spoke over their shoulders as if whispering in the lovers' ears. To New Yorkers a private-public moment on the subway like this is entirely recognizable, an almost daily occurrence.

Staging the reality of present-day young people had bugged us all along, but until now no workable solution had emerged. Following

Brecht's dictum that one should work first on the easiest thing, then the next easiest, then the next, and so on, we had kept putting it off. But now it was no longer avoidable. We tried several versions of a 1999 love scene paralleling the 1942 one, as in the improvisation, but they all came out too obvious and repetitive. Eventually we hit on the idea of some sort of song. I won't embarrass myself with examples of the discards, but suffice to say that it took several shots before the idea of rewriting the words to "Don't Sit Under the Apple Tree" arrived.

The segues into and out of the scene and the frame were finished last. The Conductor's announcement lets the audience know where we're going and why; Madame Zeitgeist's introduction sets the context and brings Yvette out into the scene; the mirroring words and gestures between Yvette and Jess establish the convention of the young woman playing the old one at an earlier time. Having Yvette watching from one side of the young couple and the young women on the other frames the scene physically and enhances the sense that Yvette is telling them the story. At the end, the elder Yvette reenters the scene before the song and after, overlaps with young Yvette, contrasting her present perspective with what she thought then, and finally walking off with her arm around her young "self."

Looking back, so many of these solutions seem so obvious. Why did it take so long and so many false starts to find them? The simple obvious solution often takes time to emerge, and working it out in a collaborative loop from the ensemble to the writer and director and back to the ensemble, around and around, is one of the most rewarding parts of the process.

Finally it is important to acknowledge that there could be many other ways to write this scene, to tell Yvette's story dramatically. This version, as you see, came from the particular personnel and dynamic of this group. You might, as an exercise, try drafting another version yourself. Or, use the transcript or the scene to provoke stories from your own group.

5

Rehearsals

Excerpt from Three Sisters and A Brother

Our version of The Three Sisters *takes place at a country home in upstate New York, where a large family has gathered to celebrate the ninetieth birthday of the oldest sister. This scene is based on the famous outburst by Irina in Chekhov—"I have forgotten everything. I can't remember the Italian for window. . . ." It was played by Etta, who was then in her late eighties and suffering from short-term memory loss, though she did learn and play this scene very successfully. Matthew is Ilyana's grandson.*

ILYANA: (*Rushes about distraught*) Where is it? Where did it go? Oh my god, I've forgotten everything. I can't remember the Russian songs my sisters sang. I can't remember my father's face. Every day I forget more and more. Life goes by and it won't ever come back. (*Looks up, sees Matt*) When did you get here?

MATTHEW: What do you mean?

ILYANA: I'm not myself these days. I'm losing my memory.

MATTHEW: You're not losing your memory. You're a wonderful storyteller.

ILYANA: Don't you sweet-talk me. I know what a charmer you are, always so nice to everyone. Well, this time it won't work.

MATTHEW: I'm not trying to charm you, Tante Ilyana. But all my life you've been telling me stories. The one about the fire. The one about the blue teakettle.

ILYANA: The blue teakettle. I must have told that story to everyone under the sun.

Matthew So, tell me a new one. Tell me about being a little girl in Russia.

ILYANA: (*Bursts out*) I don't remember!

MATTHEW: Sure you do. (*Pause*) tell me about your parents. Tell me about your brothers and sisters.

ILYANA: I don't remember. I don't remember my own father's face.

MATTHEW: (*Goes to her and kneels down at her side, so she can touch his face*) You said I looked like your father.

ILYANA: You do! You do! Every time I look at you I think of him. But what good is it when I never see you?

MATTHEW: You're seeing me right now.

ILYANA: (*Holds his face in her hands*) Am I? I suppose I am. (*Shuts her eyes. Pause*) Papa, Papa, do you remember? That time Mama was away and I was left alone with the baby? You went off on your horse to do the rounds of the estate. (*Dreamily*) Clop-clop. Clop-clop. I was so proud, so happy, keeping house just like mama. I remember the pigeons cooing and the wood smoke rising behind the barn. But then the baby started to cry. And he wouldn't stop. (*Opens her eyes, and looks with alarm into Matt's face*) He cried and cried. I thought he would die, he was crying so much. So I ran out in the fields, and I called you. "Tate! Ah, Tate!" My voice seemed so thin and frail. But somehow you heard me. And you came back. *Clop-clop. Clop-clop.* And then you were there, and you took the baby from me, and you comforted him. (*Begins to hum a fragment of a little Russian song. Smiles*) You saved my life.

MATTHEW: (*Repeats, dreamily, not mocking*) I saved your life.

ILYANA: (*Looks at him. Hums the little song again*) *That* was the song my sisters used to sing.[15]

Old Dogs Can Learn New Tricks!

"I can't learn lines!" says Selma on her first day of rehearsal. A Lower East-sider, she is earthy and funny and tough as nails. Life has beaten her up over and over, but somehow she always fights back and keeps going. Selma brought a natural stage presence, as well as some acting and dancing experience when she joined Roots&Branches. She had even starred in the Academy Award documentary *The Personals*. But the instant I handed her a script on her first day in the group, she announced, firm and loud, "I can't learn lines!"

"Sure you can," I responded, thinking she only needed some encouragement. "No, I can't! My memory is shot. I can only improvise. Give me the outlines of the scene and I'll improvise it." I knew I had a struggle on my hands.

Figure 5–1. "I've forgotten everything!" Etta Denbin, Chazz Rose, and Matthew Boline in *Three Sisters and a Brother*. Set by Tine Kindermann. Photograph by Meg Barnett.

Loss of memory is a reality of aging. And, because some kinds of memory really do slow down, many seniors give up hope of having any capacity left. It is just too frightening, too humiliating; a black hole opening before them. Avoiding the issue may be easier—as one Root was fond of saying, "Denial is not a river in Egypt."

The fear itself is often more of a problem than the actual memory loss. Fear itself is not the only thing to fear, but I do see how often fear becomes an obstacle to trying, to discovering that memory still functions, that lines and blocking can be learned and relied on.

Memory loss comes in many forms. As some kinds of memory recede, others remain fully functional, and some even seem to strengthen—it often happens that long hidden memories and skills come flooding back. Etta was an astonishing example of the unpredictability of memory. At ninety she had almost no short-term memory left; she couldn't remember if she had eaten breakfast, or what we had been talking about five minutes ago. But still, she got herself to Roots&Branches every Thursday on the bus, and, arriving early, would sit quietly doing the *New York Times* crossword puzzle in ink about as fast as she could write. She could carry on conversations in Yiddish, which she had not spoken regularly since childhood, and she had a large fund of pointed little jokes and bad puns that could be summoned on the spot.

At almost every rehearsal for a couple of years Etta would protest that she couldn't remember anything, that she was useless to the group, and couldn't understand why we wanted her there. We would insist that she was a valuable, integral, and beloved part of the group, which she was. And she was an extraordinary presence on stage, lending a special dignity, grace, slý humor, and beauty, the crown of a long, disciplined, simple life. We wanted her there, and always after some protest she would accede as if giving in to our wishes. But we knew better. She could have quit—others had when they became frail or just couldn't perform at a level that satisfied them. But she kept coming, so I knew that behind her protests was a desire to be part of the group. She also could just have come to workshops and rehearsals, and not been in the plays, but she didn't want that either. She needed the group and she needed to be useful.

For me, the key to dealing with Etta's memory issues was her ability to navigate the city bus lines. Each week she attended several evening meetings, some involving taking two or three different busses. She went alone and never got lost. How did she do this? The answer lay in a quotation I remembered from Robert Coles' great little book *The Old Ones of New Mexico*.[16] In it, Delores, an ancient farm woman says, "Habits are roads. In old age, if we have developed our habits well, they will take us where we need to go." The bus lines were a literal version of Etta's "roads." As long as she stuck to her roads, she was fine. So I made the shows into roads for her—and for everyone. I made sure that everywhere Etta had to go, there was another actor available to take her there. And to cue her on a line if need be (as always, this had to be done openly for the audience to see, because Etta was far too deaf to hear a subtle whisper). And gradually, after many rehearsals and a few performances, Etta grew less and less dependant on her helpers. Some subtle combination of visual and aural cues combined with muscle memory to get her where she needed to go. After the show she couldn't remember what had happened, but in the moment her kinetic memory and the sounds of voices saying familiar words took over and carried her through.

Selma was far from Etta's condition. Her short- and long-term memory seemed fine, but whatever loss she had experienced frightened her into thinking she couldn't possibly learn lines. Fortunately, by the time she joined the group, I had enough experience to persist in the face of her fierce resistance. And she persisted too—the thought of quitting never crossed Selma's mind. We had some pretty good fights, but in the end, our persistence won out, and she did fine in spite of her fears. Now, several years later, even after radical cancer treatments, she no longer questions her ability to learn lines, she just needs the time.

For all actors, lines and blocking are habits. We practice and practice until they are automatic, second nature. That works for the elders too. It takes longer, but it does work. The Branches learn their lines in no time, not only because of their youth, but also, as experienced actors, they are practiced at learning lines. With Selma as with others, I just keep patiently insisting that they can learn; let them stay on script for as long as possible; run lines over and over; leave a lot of time for learning lines; have them and the young actors run cues over and over; have the stage manager keep note of missed lines, so they can go over them.

When Marcy acted for the first time with us, she had never been in a play. She had little trouble understanding the scene, the character, the context, through line, motivations, and so on. Now she wanted to get her lines down pat, so she sat day and night at her kitchen table repeating the words over and over to herself. But at every rehearsal, she blanked. "They were perfect at home!" she cried. And I had to tell her what I and every other beginning actor needs to learn: "Living room perfect doesn't count."

Working with inexperienced actors, however experienced they are in other realms, demands that you articulate and repeat some basics. For example, sitting at your dining room table silently saying the lines over and over is an inefficient and generally unsuccessful way to learn lines. They have to be spoken, preferably to someone. So I have them arrange dates to cue each other in person or over the phone, as well as pairing off at rehearsal when they aren't on stage. This also helps with another rule, which is to learn the lines exactly as they are written, not approximately—the one cueing has to be a slave driver. Many beginning actors want to approximate lines—they've heard that

Brando improvised, so why can't they? In the end it is much harder to stay present if you are improvising than living in the same words every time. I tell them that if they don't like the way a line is written, they are welcome to ask for or propose a change, but otherwise they must learn it precisely. The same is true with blocking.

Blocking can be even more of a problem. Everyone knows that actors learn lines, but good actors make the blocking look so natural, so spontaneous, that it often comes as a surprise to nonactors that movement in a play is memorized behavior. In addition, many elders have not used their bodies to do more than get themselves around for years. Some have disabilities to contend with. All are slower and stiffer than they were. They envy the young's agility; sometimes feel inhibited by it, embarrassed by their own relative slowness and awkwardness. These feelings need to be countered constantly, not by false compliments, but by attention to the details of their movement, looking for movement that is possible and theatrical, by appreciating the beauty in the powerfully individual ways that elders look and move.

In 2002, David Schechter took over as lead writer/director for the season, so I could write this book. This gave me the opportunity to be more of an observer, and to think about what was going on. I watched David work with a newcomer, Ruth. Ruth had no acting experience at all. In her regular life she is organized, competent, and in control. But learning cues and blocking undid her. She seemed clueless about where to be or what to say. Even the veteran Roots were complaining, forgetting their own beginning struggles. But Ruth remained cheerful, and David, always optimistic, patient and persistent, worked with her for hours. And by the wondrous chemistry of theater, in the end, Ruth was spot on with every cue and hilarious as, variously, a beaver, good-hearted rhinoceros, and a flamingo bearing flowers.

Like lines, we run blocking again and again, until it becomes automatic. The following are some suggestions:

- **Keep Blocking Simple.** Don't drive the actors and yourself nuts trying to accomplish tricky stage movements. We always have one or two actors who, by dint of experience, natural coordination, and health, can really move as actors or dancers or both, and we exploit their skills like mad, which makes everyone look better.

110

- **There Must Be Chairs.** You can't make elders stand on stage for long periods. Hip and knee replacements, arthritis, neuropathy— there are so many reasons for avoiding standing. Often it is easier for them to move than to stand still. Because our venues may not have off-stage space, we stage our plays so that most actors are on stage all the time. So chairs or benches become integral parts of our sets.

  The actors onstage but not involved in the action, whether standing or sitting behind, are part of the scene from the audience's viewpoint. As fellow watchers, they are like a mirror for the audience, and their reactions are like cues. So we make these non-participants a sort of chorus, watching, reacting, sometimes commenting on the action, even taking sides. We choreograph the watching, cueing moments where the focus moves to the chorus for a moment, and then back to the action.

  John D. Rockefeller Sr. said, "Turn every disaster into an opportunity." It is hardly a disaster that we have to have chairs on stage and the actors present all the time, but it is a complicated necessity that we have turned into a deep part of our esthetic: the sense of the group always watching as if we are a village where everyone witnesses everything.

- **Choreography of Assistance.** Bernie can't get out of a chair without help; Molly can't hear, so she needs to be cued; Etta gets disoriented easily and needs to be led to her place. For every show we block in a choreography of assistance, which we make an explicit part of the performance. We try to relate the helping to character: so Jess, who played the Fool and Cordelia, did most of the helping of two of our Lears, Molly and Bernie, and sometimes one Lear helped another. Helping may or may not be part of the character, but it is always part of the reality of Roots&Branches, and we want the audience to see us not only as characters and actors, but as a very disparate group of people working harmoniously.

At first our audiences aren't sure what to make of all this "nonprofessional" stuff. They're not sure they are supposed to be seeing the actors helping each other. But, because the actors perform it fully, intending for it to be seen, audiences relax, and in talk-backs we get

111

lots of comments about how moving it was to see actors helping each other on stage, that it reveals how sensitive and caring young and old can be to each other. This is one of the ways we communicate what has gone on in the workshops, and through that, a feeling for what relationships between young and old can be.

Just as Brecht argued that the physical trappings of production—lights, set and costume changes, and so on—should not be hidden, so audiences are always aware that they are witnessing a performance, we argue that the physical realities of our actors and the ways we respond to them, are part of the reality the audience needs to see.

Rhythms of Learning, Moving, Stamina

As with lines and blocking, the whole process of rehearsal moves at different rates and rhythms for old and young. Our young actors are experienced and skilled, so they learn lines and blocking quickly. They are also busy students or working actors, so, even though they tend to be patient by this stage of the process, they can't hang around while elders run blocking for the umpteenth time. The solution is to rehearse a lot more with the elders than the young. Once the script is frozen and the blocking is basically set, the young actors come in once a week, and the elders two or three times.

Another aspect of aging that reveals itself in rehearsal revolves around adapting to change. I am the sort of director who has to see things to find out if they work. I am rarely able to visualize a moment so well beforehand that I can direct it in finished form the first rehearsal (I have worked with such directors, but I'm not one of them). This means I need actors who can try something, and if it doesn't work, drop it, and try something else. At any age there are actors who do well in this kind of environment and ones who don't. But the dependence on habits, combined with the power of deeply developed personalities can engender a lot of resistance to flexibility. My favorite nemesis in this realm is Muriel. Muriel learns her part better than anyone. She goes over and over lines, inflections, and blocking until she can do them exactly the same way every time. She has wonderful timing and comic sense, so when she is right, she is brilliant. But when it's not right and I want to change something, it is a struggle. Early on, we got into great contests of will, but gradually we evolved a form that works. If I ask her to change something, I say it in clear, precise language. Then Muriel repeats it back to me as a question. Then I repeat it back to her as an affirmation; and she says it yet again to confirm. Then she does it exactly as I asked, and over a few rehearsals makes it uniquely her own. But God forbid I should want to change it again!

Muriel is a particular version of the process I experience with all of the elders. Because they are such individuals, one must discover particular ways of communicating with each older actor, even more than young or middle-aged actors. In one sense their individuality makes it easier, because you aren't dealing with much pretense or wildly fluctuating personalities. Once you find the key, it's likely to remain the key.

Getting Over the Hump

One crisis we face each season occurs when the actors have to turn the stories they've told in workshops into a performance. Their original stories have often been shortened, edited, or altered. It is still a jolt to see your biography fictionalized, even if you agree that it retains the core truth and works better as theater.

Not all senior groups that work with life stories do this. The Encore Theatre of Eugene, Oregon uses the stories the elders tell as exactly as they can. Their theater is aimed at mentoring young people, many of them in trouble, and they believe that the literal truth is the best teacher. But we are aiming at a different, perhaps a more elusive kind of truth, and at different audiences for different ends. So we revise, rewrite, recast for the sake of, we hope, a deeper truth, or at least a better play.

Facing their bent autobiographies, actors sometimes protest that it didn't happen quite like that, or that something they think is crucial was left out or "He would never say it like that." Even when the story is close to the transcript, the issue still arises, because it is out of context and it may not "sound right." Sometimes people are just shocked by their own stories.

Every concern has to be taken seriously; it's part of our commitment to each other. Easy to say, but I get attached to my lovely ideas. Someone said that revision is a process of "murdering your darlings," but in this case sometimes I get them murdered for me. Every year there are one or two terrific stories that are told in workshop that can't be used in the play, because they are just too personal—illicit romances, family battles for property or hegemony, even childhood sexual abuse that happened more than seventy years ago, but still can't be spoken of above a whisper. Great stories, the stuff of drama, but when someone says no, it goes. One cliffhanger that survived was Annie's story, (see Chapter 3) about how her father banished her sister from the family when she got pregnant out of wedlock. It fit perfectly with the moment in King Lear when he banishes Cordelia. But Annie feared her family would freak when they saw it presented for all the world to see. She stewed about it, and I sweated. The positive side of the equation was time: The sister was accepted back into the family once the baby was born—"Grandchildren resolve all conflicts" is the going theory in Roots&Branches—and everyone, including the father had moved on. In the end she decided that if we changed the names, she could take the risk. And she was right. Her father was so proud of Annie and thrilled that she was in Roots&Branches, that he hardly noticed the story. Which reflects a reality of life for many: The idea that their stories are important enough to be put on stage is so unimaginable that they don't recognize themselves. Drama for them is what one sees on television or in the movies, and the only people whose stories are important are celebrities and presidents.

On matters of language or verisimilitude I tend to be more resistant to change, because theatrical truth and everyday truth are not quite the same. If Dad would never have said it that way in real life, it doesn't mean that the character "Dad" shouldn't say it that way in the play. It may take some tugging and pulling, but the actors almost always come around on this type of concern.

But there's a deeper issue: moving from telling your story to playing a character telling a story. All actors face this problem, but it is more acute when the character you are pretending to be is you and the story the character is telling or enacting is your own. As I said, the characters in our plays are often theatricalized and intensified versions of the actors, so the divide can at first seem small. Often we have to stop and talk this through.

"This is no longer your story," I have to say, "this is the character's story. It resembles, but is not exactly the same, as what happened to you. And the audience doesn't know you. What matters to them is the heart of the story, and that's what we have to create for them. You are now playing a character, who might even have the same name as you, but it's still a character." All this is well known to actors, but it is a particularly difficult process for an elderly person with a strong personality and powerful connection to the stories she tells. Eventually, everyone accepts this, at least enough so we can go on, and gradually the issue fades as the actor takes on the character and the version of the story in the play.

6

Performing

Excerpt from *Lookin' Good! A Follies*

This monologue, from our show about beauty and its role in our lives, is a charged subject when the age range is eighteen to ninety-six. It was originated by Michaela, then about seventy, but women of all ages—and many men—relate to it.

The Incredible Shrinking Woman

WOMAN: I first noticed it when I hit forty-five. The vanishing. On the streets. Men were looking right through me. I mean through me. As if I wasn't there at all. And then one day I was walking down the street with my two daughters and it was just soooo obvious. People only looked at them. No one saw me at all. I mean, at all. It was really so strange. As if I had just stepped into some other dimension where no one could see me. Just couldn't see me. As if I were suddenly actually invisible.

Now, this was the Seventies. I was reading Simone de Beauvoir and Betty Freidan, I mean, my consciousness had been raised. So, I felt a little guilty. Should this really bother me? But it did. I decided something had to be done. So, I went home and looked in the mirror. (*Takes out a little mirror; looks*) I'm still there. I'm not really invisible. Oh, my chin is getting just a little puffy. Maybe, a little brightly colored camouflage couldn't hurt. So, I looked through my things and picked out this gorgeous scarf. (*She takes a scarf from a hook upstage, puts it around her neck, and starts to cross R to L*)

Can you see me now? (*She strikes a pose while a man crosses. He doesn't notice her*)

Okay, I can't expect a silly scarf to make a big difference. It's the face. I'm getting a makeover! Don't tell my feminist friends. I'll just do it.

I left Helena Rubinstein's feeling like an exquisitely finished

Figure 6–1. Postcard advertising *Playing Lear*. Michaela Lobel as Lear. Postcard design by Anita Marlene Merk. Photograph by Elena Olivo.

canvas. A work of art that anyone with a finely developed aesthetic sense couldn't help but notice. And the city is just filled with such connoisseurs. (*Strikes a pose*) Can you see me now? (*Again a man crosses and ignores her*)

Exercise! I walk miles a day, aerobics classes, diets, vitamins, massages. I'm in great shape. My pulse is down to 60, my cholesterol is 150. I'm in great shape, but my shape is still not great.

All right. Obviously, all subtlety gets lost in the streets. This calls for radical measures! (*She considers for a moment*)

Red hair. Well, why not? (*She takes out a red wig, puts it on. Looks around, demandingly*) Well, can you see me now? (*A smile of satisfaction crosses her face*)

And it worked! Until . . . It stopped working . . . Blonde (*Replaces red wig with blonde*) . . . Ice blonde (*As before, growing more frantic*) . . . Outrageous hats (*Puts a hat on over the wig*).

Can you see me now? Can you?! Does my age make me invisible? (*Puts on a raincoat, sunglasses, so she is completely covered*) Can you see me now?[17]

It should be clear by now that performance is central to the process. Dr. Johnson said that nothing focuses the attention like the prospect of being hanged in the morning. Well, second only to that must be the prospect of performing. The certain knowledge that you and your fellow actors will be putting your butts on the line together focuses the attention of the company, and creates an atmosphere of mutual need, competition, and support. It also gives a focus to the workshops that balances and channels the necessary anarchy of our search for material.

Performing is satisfying for the company and entertains and provokes our audiences. There is a vision here of harmony between generations, a message of sorts. We enact it at many levels without pushing it, but our audiences get it and carry the message away with them.

Performing also makes the invisible visible. It has been said more than once in this book that elders are invisible in our society. In *Number Our Days*, Barbara Myerhoff reports that a member of the Senior Center in Venice, California was killed on the boardwalk by a roller skater who banged into her. "I didn't see her," he said, which led to a series of demonstrations by the members demanding that they be "seen." Having your story made into a play, then performed and watched with great interest by thousands of people is a transformative experience. Audiences too are transformed: Elders feel more visible because stories not unlike their own are made much of by being performed on stage; younger audiences experience the beauty and power of elders, and begin to notice.

Who you perform for really matters. Our elder audiences are different from the theater-savvy younger audiences that attend our benefits and off Broadway runs. At senior centers, the response can seem subdued and it is easy to think that they aren't getting it, don't like it, or are just asleep. That is rarely the case. Post-performance discussions and meet-and-greets with the actors reveal that close attention is paid by most and reactions are strong. But you won't hear them during performance to the same degree as younger audiences. My sense is that elders react from different places in themselves than younger audiences—experience, memory, and standards of judgment and decorum (for or against) matter more to elders. They are less willing to accept things at face value or to follow trends. Newness matters less than memory. When the self is more past than future, containing vast reservoirs of experience and feeling, the present is engaged from a different place than when one is age twenty or fifty.

Touring

Roots&Branches performs at senior centers, schools, and community centers during the day. Often there is no formal stage; we are in a general purpose room with the audience on the same level as we are. Or in a lunch room with the tables pushed back and some rows of chairs and the kitchen staff clanging pots in the background. There might be a huge stage in a large auditorium with poor acoustics or a tiny platform that makes our large cast feel like they are in an elevator. The point is that we have to stage our plays simply and flexibly so we can tour on a shoestring, and perform under almost any circumstances.

But we also have to make our shows theatrical, so a lot of imagination goes into sets and props. We have used backdrop flats for years. They are simple to carry and assemble and can evoke a lot. For *Playing Lear*, Dawn Robyn Petrlik designed an evocatively decrepit proscenium arch that came apart so it could be carried easily in a van. When *Lear* characters appeared, they came through the arch, when they were present-time characters, they entered elsewhere. We also bought a dozen green plastic patio armchairs ($6 apiece), which created a kind of court on either side of the arch. It was simple, set the scene, provided the necessary chairs, and were light and easy to stack and carry. When we were finally in a theater and could use lights, the effect was spectacular.

David Schechter is a marvel at making much of little. This year for *Growing Up/Growing Down* he assembled piles of small objects—stuffed animals, dolls, toys, posters, costume pieces, completely indescribable things—that made a fairy world of wonder and silliness in just the right proportions.

Our Company Manager for the last four years, Lauren Scott, now also a member of the ensemble, makes detailed arrangements with the venues far ahead of our arrival. We need to know whatever we can about the space and the audience, and to let them know the arrangements we need. Any theater on tour has basic needs—load-in and out access, electricity, performance space, and so on—and we have added

Figure 6–2. *Growing Up/Growing Down* (2003). Lauren Scott in center; clockwise from lower left: Yvette Pollack, Marcy Ried, Zoe Lister-Jones, Esther Horne, Deena Selenow. Props by David Schechter. Photograph by Elena Olivo.

ones because we are traveling with elders. Obviously access must be clear and simple. Restrooms need to be nearby.

And there is *lunch*. The young can skip a meal or two with no significant effect, but for elders, regular meals, on schedule are often a medical necessity, and are certainly necessary when preparing to put out the energy a performance demands. So Lauren makes sure that there is some arrangement for eating. Sometimes the center serves lunch, so we ask that they put aside lunches for us and make sure we can get them when we need them—if the center is serving a hundred or more lunches, that can take some arranging. If no lunch is served, we make sure that everyone brings food or that we can order in.

We send some promotional materials and make sure that the audiences know something about us. Before each performance, David Schechter or I introduce the company to the audience explaining that Roots&Branches is an intergenerational company, and describing our process a bit, so audiences know that the play they are going to see is based on true stories from the lives of the performers. It's important that our audiences have some context, a subject to be discussed more in the next chapter.

When we can, the cast and directors gather with the audience after the show and respond to comments and questions. Our plays usually provoke memories for our audiences and this is the time to share them. It's also a chance for the actors and audience to bond in an informal way, and to deepen the sense of the value of connections between generations.

7

Toward an Esthetic of Community-Based Theater

Excerpt from *Playing Lear* (A redacted version of a couple of scenes)

(*Lear is living in Goneril's castle with his entourage of 100 knights, which he demanded as part of agreeing to give up his crown. Things are not going well . . .*)

GONERIL: Not only, sir, this your all-licensed fool,
    But other of your insolent retinue
    Do hourly carp and quarrel, breaking forth
    In rank and not-to-be-endured riots.
    I had thought by complaining of this to you
    That you would impose discipline and manners
    On your men, but you do nothing.
    You have too many knights!
    I implore you then a little to disquantity your train,
    Or I will be forced to do it for you.
LEAR: Darkness and devils!
    I still have a daughter left; I'll go to her.
    Degenerate bastard, I'll not trouble thee;
    Hear, Nature, hear; dear Goddess, hear!
    Into her womb convey sterility,
    Or, if she must breed, create her child of spleen;
    Let it stamp wrinkles in her brow, so she may feel
    How sharper than a serpent's tooth it is
    To have a thankless child! Away, away! (*Lear and Fool exit*)
MARTHA: Why does Lear need so many knights?
BERNIE: He thinks that without his 100 knights he would be but a
    walking shadow.

ANNIE: It's like my grandmother with her kitchen. She refuses to give up her huge kitchen and all her pots and pans, even though she has no one to cook for any more.

ESTHER: That's how it was with my mother and her high-heeled shoes. She kept wearing them, even when she was eighty years old. She insisted on it, until finally, she began to fall down.

Martha as Esther's mother totters in on high heels.

So I said, "Mom, you have to stop wearing high heels. You're going to kill yourself. Please, wear these sensible shoes."

MOTHER: Sensible shoes!

Kneels and starts to change her mother's shoes.

ESTHER: But, Mother, you don't need high heels.

LEAR/MOTHER: Oh, reason not the need!

LEAR: I can be patient, I can stay with Regan,
I and my hundred knights.

REGAN: Not altogether so. What, fifty followers?
I entreat you to bring but twenty-five.
To no more will I give place or notice.

LEAR: I gave you all.

REGAN: And in good time you gave it.

LEAR: What must I come to you with twenty-five?

REGAN: And speak't again, father, no more with me.

LEAR: (*Turns to Goneril*)
I'll go with thee.
Thy fifty yet doth double twenty-five.
So you do love me twice again as much.

GONERIL: Hear me, father.
What need you five-and-twenty? Ten? Or five?

REGAN: What need you one?

LEAR: Oh, reason not the need!
Our basest beggars
Are in the poorest things superfluous
Allow not nature more than nature needs,
Man's life is cheap as beast's.

MARCY: I can't stop trying to think what my 100 knights will be.

What will that nice young social worker be trying to convince me
to part with so she can get me in the van that's taking me to the
nursing home?

MURIEL: Talking makes me, me. If my hands stopped working and I
couldn't write, I would still be me, but if I couldn't talk, then they
could cart me off to the glue factory.

MICHAELA: Independence! That's my hundred knights. If I couldn't
take care of myself, take a walk, participate in my activities, I
don't think I would want to live.

ANNIE: My work is my hundred knights. I love being busy; having
people depend on me, respect me. When I'm not working, I'm lost.

YVETTE: Y'know, I don't think I know what my hundred knights will
be. It might surprise me. My father's certainly did. He had this
fantastic card memory. He could remember every hand, every card
he ever played. Then one night suddenly he couldn't remember
. . . even the cards he just played. That's how the mind works, I
guess. And he never played cards again.[18]

The Good Enough Mother and the 100 Knights

There is a widespread tendency to defend or promote community-
based theater on the grounds that we make good process and politics
and, therefore, the esthetics are either unimportant or that we can't be
judged by the esthetics of regular theater. This is nonsense. As Louis
Armstrong said, "There's only two kinds of music; good and bad." The
same is true of theater. Bad theater does nothing but undermine the
values we promote.

Still, there are real differences between what we do and commercial
theater, not-for-profit professional theater or experimental theater,
and we need to examine the differences in terms of the opportunities
they provide for creating something unique and valuable.

We go to different theaters with different desires and for different
satisfactions. Not long ago, in one week I saw *Vienna Lusthaus* by
Martha Clark at New York Theatre Workshop, and the Broadway
revival of Michael Frayn's *Noises Off*. I brought very different expectations to each, and came away satisfied (or not) in very different
ways. *Vienna Lusthaus* is a downtown dance/theater piece about high

art, deep psychology, and heavy politics; *Noises Off* is pure farce, a magic act, all skill and timing, about a micro-millimeter deep, and if anyone in it tried for one instant to be sincere or profound, you would want to punch them. If I judged *Noises Off* by the same standards as *Vienna Lusthaus*, I would be a fool.

But how do we judge Roots&Branches or any community-based theater? The problem is that no one quite yet knows. The field is fairly new and there is a wide range of content, styles, and skills. While we would be setting ourselves up for disappointment to look for Broadway-level performances and production values, we also must not forgive embarrassing acting or writing or production. So what do we have a right to expect and demand?

Roots&Branches plays, or any community-based art, should offer entrée into worlds we have not yet seen in the mainstream—insights, stories, history, subject matter, attitudes, worldviews, politics. There are many examples in our work, and the excerpt at the beginning of this chapter is a good one. The question of why Lear insists upon his 100 knights so vehemently is simply never raised in any Shakespeare criticism I have read.[19] Several commentators suggest that Lear is keeping a small but significant army to ensure his fair treatment by his daughters, whom he has reason to suspect. Or it is just assumed that 100 knights are a perquisite of kingship that he clings to irrationally and it is left at that. Nowhere could I find any discussion of the 100 knights in reference to Lear's great age.

Letting go is perhaps the defining experience of aging. First may be work, which for many is the defining element of their lives. In the generation that is aged now, it is still mostly men for whom that is true, and it is common at senior centers to see the few men there, hanging around listlessly as the women maintain vigorous social lives and activities. These days many retired people take up new careers or attack hobbies with all the vigor they put into their careers. But as time goes on "the descent beckons," as William Carlos Williams writes, and one activity after another must be cut back or given up—work, home, driving, travel, entertaining, vigorous exercise. At each point there is a struggle and mourning and eventually acceptance and adaptation to new definitions of independence and self. When my aunt could no longer drive she used her considerable skills at conversation and intimacy to entice people to offer to take her shopping. She had people lined up for weeks, and thus managed to maintain her independence for years.

Anyone who is aging or around aged people knows all about this, but it had never, as far as I can tell, come up in reference to *King Lear*. However, when I proposed to the group the notion that Lear clings to his 100 knights partly because he senses that without them he would no longer be himself, recognize himself, and asked, "What is your 100 knights; what is it that if you lost it, you would no longer recognize yourself, would no longer be yourself?" the Roots picked up on this immediately, telling stunning stories, mostly about their parents and grandparents. (Not about themselves for two reasons, I think: First, they can't know. Who would have guessed that high heels would be the breaking point for an old woman, certainly not her daughter. Secondly, it is just too hard, too close to the bone to dwell on this issue for long, when it is an approaching reality.)

Interestingly, the notion of what one would irrationally hold on to as a definer of yourself became a constant topic of discussion among young as well as old. When she was moving to Germany after graduation, Sabine told us that she just wouldn't part with her white shirts. She had something like thirteen white shirts, and her friends were urging her to get rid of some. But she couldn't do it, she said, "I love white shirts, they say who I am better than any other clothes. Those shirts are my 100 knights." Even a high school student wrote to us that the 100 knights section made him think of the window in his room, which had looked out over a nice view, which now was being blocked out by a new building going up next door. For him it referenced something lost and never to be recovered.

This is one instance among many in which the perspectives of generations and aging came up with something genuinely original. And that should be a fundamental goal of a community-based theater—to see with new eyes, because of a unique perspective. African American theater, women's, and gay theater have all accomplished this to the point where many of their once startling and controversial perspectives and insights are now mainstream.

What can Roots&Branches communicate that mainstream theater can't, or can't yet? This question drives many of our esthetic choices.

Figure 7–1. Bernie Basescu as Lear; Jessica Burr as the Fool, *Playing Lear* (2002). Photograph by Elena Olivo.

For example, in *Playing Lear*, we could have cast one woman, Michaela, as Lear. She has the power and the acting skills to make a powerful Lear. But in fact there have been several female Lears in recent years, and aside from her greater age, it would have been nothing particularly striking or revelatory of Lear or Roots&Branches. So instead we chose to have four different people play Lear, each expressing an aspect, a facet of this infinite character.

At the beginning of the play when Lear divides his kingdom, we cast Bernie. Bernie has Parkinson's disease, which now pretty much confines him to a wheelchair. His hands shake and he cannot count on his voice to project above a near whisper. So he certainly suggests a very frail old man. As a friend wrote, "this casting gives me a sense of how terrifying and frustrating it must be for an old man to give up his power; to have to depend for the first time since childhood upon the love and honor of others rather than authority and might. I think of my father. And of myself in some too rapidly approaching future."[20]

But Bernie also has a bearded brooding face, a perfect visage for Lear, and a wise and gentle manner. Lear must have been a good king before he began to lose it, because all the good guys like him and all the bad guys hate him. So having this frail, gentle soul play Lear at the beginning made him seem not only old, but also sympathetic. Then, when he turns on Cordelia, revealing the incursion of what we might today call dementia, the moment is at least in part about age, as opposed to the more standard interpretation of a tyrant who, as Regan says, "hath ever but little known himself."

Michaela presented Lear in his petulance and rage. She has the volcanic power and the acting skills to be truly frightening, and the moment when she curses Goneril, circling her and pointing at her womb, was doubly chilling because it was also a woman cursing another woman.

When Lear's daughters drive home his impotence by taking all of his knights away, we had twenty-two-year-old Annie in the role. The frame of the play was a rehearsal of a new production of *King Lear*, and Annie played the rather arrogant young director taking out her anger at her father by shaping the show to emphasize Lear's arrogance and irrationality and the daughters' good sense (if a bit excessively and coldly applied). At this point in the rehearsal, the actors gang up on her and insist she play Lear in this scene to experience the helplessness of great age and frailty. When Regan says, "What need you one [knight]," and Lear cries, "Oh, reason not the need . . ." the young director finally gets it that reason is not always the best or only criterion.

In the storm, Michaela howled Lear's rant—"Blow, winds, and crack your cheeks . . ." —while ninety-six-year-old Molly shrieked and battered the air with her fists behind her. Anyone who saw that image of great age ranting at fate would agree it was indelible.

The three aged Lears—Bernie, Molly, and Michaela—come together to beg forgiveness of the returned Cordelia, and then, when Lear and Cordelia are captured and bound, Molly speaks the great speech in which Lear sublimely envisions perfect freedom in maximum limitation ("Come, let us away to prison, and we two shall sing like birds i' the cage"), which Helen M. Luke describes as one of the most sublime evocations of the pure wisdom of great age.[21]

What other theater could evoke the variety of Lear's humanity, and ours, in this way? Obviously there are infinite ways, but we found one that made use of our strengths, reflected our focus on age and intergenerational issues, and offered original insights and images. This is what we seek and it should be part of any measure of community-based art.

Roots&Branches also seeks to communicate a sense of community, intimacy, possibility, and transformation that might only come from the lived experience of an ensemble of people who really are what they are pretending to be on stage. And this would apply to many senior and other theaters that use their own stories. There is something different about a theater in which actors are telling themselves from one in which actors are performing others' stories. It is hard to articulate, but it can be felt in Roots&Branches in the passion of the telling, the sense of truth, and urgency in the actors—they are not doing this for fame or fortune (though none would turn those down); they want you to know them, to hear their stories. The choreography of helping described in Chapter 5 is another facet of evoking the unique ambience of Roots&Branches, along with the content and style of the work, and the simple fact of such a wide range of ages working joyously and well together. As one rather hardened veteran of the New York theater scene put it, "I don't know why, but every time I see a Roots&Branches production, I come away feeling so happy."

But what about performance and production levels? What do we have a right to expect? To demand?

Let's get the chops question out of the way immediately. Our acting and production values—and those of community-based theater in general—are not up to Hollywood, Broadway, off-Broadway or most off-off standards. Period! We should not pretend otherwise. There are lots of reasons. Some are practical, including lack of training and experience, money, rehearsal time, and so on. And some are ideological; we have agendas other than pure art, such as community-building or bringing a message of understanding and links between the generations. We treasure the authenticity of people telling their own stories. But these good values don't exempt us from the responsibility to make our plays theatrical and enjoyable to watch. It's just that if we start seeking high art standards, we are off-track and wasting everybody's time. The pleasures and treasures to be had here are elsewhere.

So, how should we measure the acting and production values of Roots&Branches and other senior and community-based theaters? The psychologist D. W. Winnicott had a concept he called *the good enough mother*. Writing in the 1950s, a time when motherhood was under heavy fire from the therapeutic community, Winnicott argued that the child played a role in its own development, and that mothers don't have to be perfect, they have to be "good enough" not to interfere with the child's natural proclivity to develop healthily. Basically, a mother is good enough when she doesn't get in the way. As a single father I liked that idea, and I like that idea as an esthetic for Roots&Branches.

The acting and production values should at minimum be good enough. Good enough to keep your interest; good enough to entertain; good enough to trigger the imagination; good enough to communicate the substance, spirit, and vision of the moment and the play. Good enough to dignify the cause, the subject, the writers, the directors, the actors, and so on. Good enough to feel like theater. Obviously how one judges all this is subjective, but so are all criteria. It does, however, set realistic goals on many levels and allows us to get on with the work and the watching.

In the case of Roots&Branches, we discovered early on that most people come to senior theater somewhat as they come to the school

Figure 7–2. Ida Harnden dancing, Chazz Rose and Clarence Carter in background. Set by Tine Kindermann. Photograph by Lisa B. Segal.

plays of their children. Like school plays, many attend, not because they expect to see a good show, but rather out of a sense of obligation—to someone in the show or to the idea of senior theater. They

131

expect amateurish performances, and a kind of goofy, charming, and "up with people" sentimentality. This may sound harsh, but it's true, and in this harsh truth lies our opportunity. Given such low expectations, all we have to do to astonish and delight our audiences is significantly exceed their expectations. And we dance in that space between audience expectations and what we deliver. Roots&Branches shows have content that challenges, surprises, and moves, and production values that far exceed expectations. In other words, we are *good enough.*

Once the audience has a context, including knowledge of the group, its intentions, style, and means, and some cultural understanding or even common ground, they can receive, enjoy, and criticize the work with their full subjectivity.

Community-based theater, still in its infancy in terms of the history of theater, has generated some scholarly interest and in a few cases some respect from the larger theater community, but we have a long way to go, most of us, before we enter the public dialogue.

Afterword

Barbara Myerhoff introduced me to the idea of communicating with the dead through imagined conversations and letters. In *Number Our Days*, she writes letters to her beloved friend Shmuel, who died while the work was in progress. She knew him so well, she could hear his voice. Over the eighteen years since Barbara died, I have kept a photo and some other tokens of our friendship, and she has always been there over my left shoulder nudging me on with this work, with my life. I do try to talk to her from time to time, and sometimes she's there. As I finish this book, she is very present, asking, "So, what have you personally learned from all this?" Others have asked this too, so I'll put my response in the form of a letter to Barbara.

Dear Barbara:

When I started Roots&Branches I was forty-nine years old. Now I am sixty-two. So this is what I did with my fifties. Part of it. At forty nine I was firmly planted in middle age. I was neither Root nor Branch. Now I get Senior discounts; now I've been a member of AARP for more than a decade. Now the Roots ask me, "So when are you going to join us?"

In *Number Our Days*, you say you studied the old Jews of Venice, California, not only as an anthropologist, but also as a Jewish woman looking ahead to her own aging. Studying old Jews was very different from studying your earlier anthropological subject, the Huichol Indians. Because, you said, while you could never become a Huichol Indian, you would one day be a little old Jewish lady. That never happened—you died at the age I was when I started Roots&Branches. But you couldn't know that, so you watched these old women and men with what you called "reflexive" interest, the interest of one who needs to know for herself as well as for her job. How did they deal with the struggles of old age? What made them so grittily determined to keep going in spite of illness, crippling degeneration of joints and muscles, loss of hearing, sight, memory, taste, and touch? And most of all death, the death of family, friends, and the ever growing imminence of their own? How do they do it?

When I started Roots&Branches the impulse came from a social concern. I saw how segregated our culture is by generations and how much is missing because of that, and I wanted to do something. Now my interest is more personal. Like you, I want to learn some things about how to do the next couple of stages of my life, if I am lucky enough to live them out. And there you are, parked insistently over my left shoulder, asking again, "So, nu, what have you learned?"

First of all, I am aging all the time, not just learning about something in the future, so the best learning is the week in week out interaction with all these people, of all these ages. I am constantly forced to look at what I think I know and see that from the perspective of someone much younger or older it ain't the same. A play I love means nothing to Jennifer, or to Esther either. And I have to tell myself over and over, they're not wrong. Jessica says I have to see some new experimental breakthrough, and I find I've seen it all before, but try to love it through her eyes. Or Yvette tells me about the reunion of the veterans of the Spanish Civil War with tears in her eyes and angry pride in her voice, and I listen lovingly, but it's all as ancient history to me as Vietnam is to Zoe and Deena. And they bring out all the ages that are in me. My body may be sixty-two, but in me are all those ages I've been and the imagining of all I will be. And they come out in workshops, because they are all around me.

Most of what I hope I've learned is so simple seeming, so obvious, almost cliché sounding. But so hard to do. Etta at ninety-two, doing her ten minutes a day of exercise—alternate nostril breathing, lifting her arms, twisting at the waist, standing first on one foot, then the other. And then the crossword puzzle for her mind. That doesn't sound hard. But every day, every single day, no matter how she felt, no matter what. Every day. That's the hard part. "Don't you get bored?" I want to ask. And I hear her high humorous voice: "You either like it or lump it." She'd had a tough life, much of it lonely and never financially better than getting by. And what she'd learned, what kept her dignity and earthy humor intact, was, "You either like it or lump it."

I'm not comfortable with that, but I know it will serve me well as my body inevitably lets go.

These elders exude their determined courage to be in life. Bernie, with advancing Parkinson's, gets himself there, which takes more determination and discipline each time than it has taken me to write this book. Where will I get that? I don't know, but I have to look hard.

I have watched so many elders, even in my own family, just quit, just grow bitter or passive and narrow. But these ones never stop. Knowing they can't compete with their young selves, even if they want to, they take up new challenges, learn new lines, meet new people, take on new causes. They want life. They want freedom. And if freedom means adjusting to new limitations, well so be it. Can't run around so much? Well learn the Internet and get online. And find young friends to take you shopping. Can't garden as big a patch as you could before? Well start a window box. Freedom has as many definitions as we can imagine.

Another learning that takes constant reinforcement for me is the power of doing something for the sheer love of it, and this I watch in both generations. The Roots have no reason to come to workshop every week, learn their lines and blocking and then shlep out to unglamorous venues and perform their hearts out. No reason but their love for the work and each other. They do get some fame. Michaela is regularly recognized as she walks on upper Broadway or in the grocery store, and she calls me every time, so we can celebrate her celebrity together. And perhaps that is compensation enough. Some, like Michaela, come more for the acting, some more for the group. Molly repeats over and over, "Every week you people save my life!" Hyperbolic perhaps, which is, after all, Molly's way, but there are always several nods of agreement, including sometimes, mine. And the Branches too, are here for love. In school or recently out, they are anything but hardened, no matter how tough they appear. They are in theater for the love of it. They exude that love and enthusiasm, and it infects all of us. Of course they have high ambitions and dreams, and of course their careers matter. But Roots&Branches, while it gives them a place to practice their craft and some solid training in ensemble technique, can't be worth the time it demands in career terms.

And community, a word so easily bandied about. I have attended workshops and conferences, listened to learned speeches, and read books on the subject. But somehow, Barbara, I learn more from Ida, who would make sure that everyone in the group got a hug as they came in. It was silly, and coming from anyone other than this tiny eighty-year-old fireplug, I might have resisted. But it eased the entrance. And the shmooze time; half an hour of just socializing, with a little food, before we get down to work. The work itself, building an atmosphere of charged intimacy, never the same from week to week, but predictably focused and with common elements that make it familiar enough. And the careful networking that some of the Roots carry on, checking in on each other, getting the news, venting, just touching base. It all works to make our group, which is widely dispersed around the city and living very disparate lives, something like a community or a village or a family. Not any of those, exactly, some new synthesis, that works for us in this time and place.

I learned in childhood the intense temporary community that being in a play creates and I loved it. But then it ended and you had to start all over again. It was the genius of Joe Chaikin and a few others who saw that this intensity could be extended and worked with not only to keep people together longer, but to produce theater made from the lives and imaginations of the participants. So this letter is to you too, Joe.

The lessons aren't hard to know intellectually. The value for me is in the continuing exposure. Maybe, by being around this quotidian greatness week in week out, I will learn it by the same osmosis that we learn language or morals or eating habits.

I don't know if I'll age better for all this time spent with the youthful Roots and the wise old Branches. But I sure have models, and I'm better for it all the same. So thank you, Barbara and Joe, for being my tap roots. Keep talking to me, please.

Love,
Arthur

Appendix 1

An Anthology of Roots&Branches Scenes

Throughout the text, there have been excerpts from plays. Each chapter opens with one, and several more are used as examples within chapters. They are as much a part of this Anthology as the scenes that follow. Included here are monologues—two- and three-person scenes. There are larger group scenes in the book.

The scenes can be read and acted as written, and I think actors will find challenge and pleasure in that. They can also be springboards for discussion, improvisation, and play development of your own. Please see the discussions of scene and play development in the text for guidelines on how to go about that.

*Monologues**

Housecleaning
(From *It's About Time!*)[22]

Ida Harnden, who originated this monologue, was a very energetic eighty-year-old former vaudeville dancer. She was all over the stage during this piece, demonstrating how she controls the mess. The monologue offers the opportunity to break the stereotype of slow-moving old people with a lot of comedic movement.

IDA: I have less time these days, because my energy lasts for just so long. And I use it all outside the house. I enjoy my family, my

---

*Another monologue appears on p. 116.

friends, my theater group, my organizations. I'm overinvolved and I love it. But by the time I get home, I'm exhausted.

So I have evolved a system so I can do everything I want. I don't clean my house! . . . I'm clean. I take showers. It's just my house I don't clean.

I have one room. I call it my "What the hell am I gonna do with this?" room. I have papers from twenty years ago. One of these days I'm gonna get to them; one of these days. For now (*picking up imaginary papers and tossing them*) They go into the "What the hell am I gonna do with this?" room. Letters, pamphlets, things to be ironed, things to be hemmed, bottles to be returned, my goodwill bag. You know, the "I must get to it someday" stuff. Into the room, close the door, and there it stays until . . . someday.

Company? No problem. Where does company go? The living room. Okay, I take all the piles in the living room, shove them in the "What the hell am I gonna do with this?" room and close the door! The kitchen? I just tell them, "I don't like help in my kitchen." Why put away dishes you use every day? That's what dish drains are for!

The bedroom? Shove everything into the closet and close the door tight. Any snoops who open closets or doors do so at their own risk, and will be too embarrassed to talk about it. . . . I hope!

Deep breathing is very healthy. Take a really deep breath. (*Gets audience to join her*) Now exhale. There goes the dust!

Floors? Don't even think about getting down on your knees and scrubbing. And don't use a mop. Just get strong paper towels, splash floor cleaning stuff on the floor, wet the towels, spread 'em on the floor and skate!

The "Skater's Waltz" comes up, and she skates around the floor, with pirouettes, arabesques.

END

Millie's Monologue from *It's About Time!*

Elders live with illness and death as shadow companions, but they are very difficult to bring to our theater. Millie Gold had the extraordinary courage to tell her story of a twenty-year struggle with cancer, then work with me for weeks to craft this monologue, and then to perform it over and over. It had a huge impact and Millie performed it as a solo piece many times, including at Golda's Place, a center in New York for women with cancer. The song she sings had particular resonance for her, but another, that works for you could be substituted.

Millie enters L singing an old melancholy Yiddish love song. She breaks off.

Let me tell you about time. I know something about time.

All sit in semicircle around Millie.

MILLIE: I have to confess that time and I have been, well, having a very special relationship for fifteen years. Sometimes we are as close and intimate as lovers; sometimes we are at each other's throats, but it is never casual or light.

It wasn't always like that. Time and I used to be pretty free and easy. When I was young, time was my friend. Time was on my side. My parents said, "Go to college. Stay at home with us." But I said, "No, I don't need college. I need freedom. I need to sing."

(*Sings*) Oh, freedom, oh, freedom
  Oh, freedom over me

But I wasn't stupid. I knew how to support myself. My office skills gave me a living, but songs, friends, and lovers gave me life. Then the time came when I was ready to go to college. I loved it. I loved it so much I even went on to graduate school. I had a whole new life planned out for myself.

(*Sings*) I'm on my way, and I won't look back
  I'm on my way, and I won't look back

But time doesn't work like that. A few months before I graduated, I went for my annual check up. I'm a great believer in preventive medicine. When I left the doctor's office, time was at my throat. My whole past was wiped out. All I could think or remember or see was the doctor telling me I had a malignant tumor in my left breast.

Sings Yiddish song, "Mein Hartz Weint in Mir"
Mein hartz, mein hartz, weint in mir
Az ich darf mich sheidn itzt mit dir,
Maine gedanken ahin aher,
Mit dir tzu sheidn iz mir shver.
(My heart, my heart, cries in me
That I must part from you
My thoughts are here and there
Being with you is hard for me)

Or was it my right breast. Sometimes it's hard to remember. I was forty-four years old, and they wanted my left breast. But I'm a *starker*, the show must go on. So I had the surgery, finished graduate school, and went to work. I had a plan and I wasn't going to let cancer get in the way. Three years later, I went for my regular checkup. And there went the second breast.

Sings crazily while doing wall climbing exercise:
Abba dabba dabba dabba dabba dabba dabba,
Said the monkey to the chimp.
Abba dabba dabba dabba dabba dabba dabba,
Said the chimpey to the monk

I'm climbing walls. That's what you do after you have a mastectomy. You put your fingers on the wall and you walk up like this. Because you have to build up strength and flexibility. After a mastectomy, you climb walls.

But after the second breast was gone, I wanted to be whole, so I had reconstructive surgery. When I came out of the hospital, I looked, and really felt beautiful. (*Sings mein hertz and dances and strokes her arms, shoulders, neck. Sustain this image into next section.*) Time backed off a little. We were in a truce.

Six months later I was rubbing cream on my body after my bath, and I discovered a lump right here. The doctor did a biopsy on the lump and told me I had something called non-Hodgkin's lymphoma. I had never even heard of non-Hodgkin's lymphoma. And my doctor told me, "I can't treat you any more. You have to go to these new doctors, who specialize in this condition." It was like losing a lover.

Sings from "Mein Hertz"
Vu forstu main zis lebn
Vu forstu fun mir avek?
(where are you going, beloved
where are you going, away from me)
I sing these love songs to myself.

Right at that moment I was offered a wonderful job. But I would have to take a lot of time off for treatment, and there were problems about changing insurance. I couldn't do it. I had to build everything around treatment and insurance. Cancer was my new career.

Sings "Mein Hertz"
Vu vel ich dich dortn zuchn
Zog-zhe mir, oif veichn veg?
(where will I see you
tell me, which way)

(*Resumes rubbing*) So I had the radiation and the chemo, and I lost my hair. And then I was all right for a couple of years. And then I found another lump—here, or was it here? I can't always remember which one came when. More radiation, more chemo, less hair. And then a couple of years of, well, not quite health, not quite freedom, more like waiting. More like doing the best I could with the time I had until the next lump, the next chemo, the next god damned wig.

Sings reprise of "Mein Hertz"

My doctors love me. I'm their best patient. I do everything right, and I keep surviving—that's the part they like best. I love them too. They're my lovers now.

When I'm going through the treatments, all I am is the sickness and the treatment. But when it's done I want to have fun. I live

141

for passions and feelings. I live for the moment—the moment is all I've got. I go to movies or shows you don't have to buy tickets for months in advance. I go out to dinner on a moment's notice. I relish every moment with friends. My favorite time words are *moment, instant, now,* and, yes, *remember.* I hate words like *later, then,* and especially *future.* I'm more selective now. I don't plan trips. I walk away from fools.

Time, you have taught me what I'm made of. I would never have known if you hadn't dealt me this new career. But don't ask me to thank you.

Every day I take a bath and after I rub cream all over my body. It feels wonderful, but it's also how I find the new lumps. My hair is coming in nicely this time. And I'm getting gray hair. I'm so proud of it.

She sings "dortn, dortn" *as she goes to L bench and is embraced by Ida.*
Oy dayne oygelech, vi di shvartse kershelech
Un dayne lipelech, vi rozeve papir
Un dayn fingerlech, vi tint un feder
Oy, shraybn zolstu ofte briv tsu mir
(oh your eyes like black cherries
and your lips, a rosy moon
and your fingers, pen and ink
oh, write to me often and soon)

END

Two-Person Scenes*

Rudy and Jeanette, A Love Scene
From *Romeo & Juliet and Juliet & Romeo and Romeo & Juliet*[23]

RUDY, a retired ad executive, and JEANETTE, a successful writer of romance novels, meet during the Shakespearean cruise on the luxury liner S.S. Verona. They discover much in common—they are New Yorkers; love literature, theater, and music; and they are both sophisticated and witty. To their surprise, they fall in love. They thought they were done with all that. Now the cruise is nearly over, and they have to decide their star-crossed fate.

It is just before dawn; Rudy and Jeanette are on the deck, standing by the railing, looking out at moon over the waves.

RUDY: (*Sings*) Two sleepy people by dawn's early light.
    And too much in love to say good night.
JEANETTE: (*Quotes Juliet*) "Wilt thou be gone? It is not yet near day
    It was the nightingale and not the lark,
    That pierced the fearful hollow of thine ear."
RUDY: "It was the lark, the herald of the morn
    No nightingale."
JEANETTE: "Yond light is not daylight; I know it.
    Therefore stay yet, thou need'st not be gone."
RUDY: I *am* a little bit tired.
JEANETTE: "Thou knowest the mask of night is on my face."
RUDY: Let's talk; it's not day. You were right. It *was* the nightingale,
    not the lark.
    "I am no pilot; yet, wert thou as far
    As that vast shore washed with the farthest sea
    I should adventure for such merchandise."
JEANETTE: You're so funny.
RUDY: "Thinks't we shall ever meet again?"

---

*See pp. 8, 59, 61, and 105 for more two-person scenes.

143

JEANETTE: "I must hear from thee every day in the hour
For in a minute there are many days."
RUDY: "Come live with me and be my love." (*Pause*)
JEANETTE: You're not serious.
RUDY: I'm very serious.
JEANETTE: You'd get annoyed with me and want me to go away.
You'd start fights over little things.
RUDY: I . . . wouldn't.
JEANETTE: You would and you wouldn't tell me why.
RUDY: (*Sighs*) We're both such individuals.
JEANETTE: My independence is my life. (*Pause*)
Disappointed?
RUDY: (*Melodramatic*) "I dreamt my love came and found me dead."
JEANETTE: You're not *that* disappointed.
RUDY: Actually, I'm relieved. I can listen to my opera recordings
anytime. And I can live in the disorder I love. (*Pause*)
JEANETTE: You're messy. I'm neat.
I have my schedule. Three pages a night.
RUDY: You work late?
JEANETTE: And I sleep late.
RUDY: I'm an early riser. Always up for breakfast.
Out with friends 'til late at night.
JEANETTE: Lots of peace and quiet works for me.
I unplug my phone when I want to be alone.
RUDY: I'm on the phone day and night. My light is always on even
when I sleep.
JEANETTE: I sleep in total darkness. I like the lights out.
RUDY: Day and night.
JEANETTE: Sweet and sour.
RUDY: I say either.
JEANETTE: I say *either*.
RUDY AND JEANETTE: (*Sing together*) Let's call the whole thing off.

Pause—they laugh.

RUDY: Is there any way we could get along?
JEANETTE: We could make time between your phone calls and my
silences.

RUDY: (*Mulling it over*) make time—part-time.

JEANETTE: When I need to be alone, I want to be *alone*. But when I want company you could be my man.

RUDY: Anytime I'm available. I'd make lots of room for you.

JEANETTE: I like to sleep alone. . . . Most of the time. How about afternoon trysts?

RUDY: Daylight is not my element. Love in the light is not for me. There's too much sin in it. I need the cover of darkness.

JEANETTE: We could meet at twilight. That's an exciting and mysterious time. Anything is possible then.

RUDY: Twilight trysts. Wow! I've never tried that. (*Pause*) Let's take it slowly.

JEANETTE: We could go away weekends or on another cruise.

RUDY: I'd like that. (*Pause*) But I don't want any surprise visits.

JEANETTE: Don't worry. And I'm not giving you my keys, either.

RUDY: Then we can be friends . . . forever.

JEANETTE: I'd like that . . . forever.

Music—a distant waltz.

RUDY: We'll dance the night away.(*Takes her in his arms*)

JEANETTE: We can agree on that.

RUDY: "O, wilt thou leave me so unsatisfied?"

JEANETTE: No! (*She kisses him*)

END

Old AIDS
(From *I Am Acting My Age!*)[24]

As the scene opens, Rose is trying on some old hats she found in a closet and dancing to music on the radio. The hats are on a kitchen table with two chairs. Charlie enters, agitated.

CHARLIE: Rose, I'm home. (*Sits*)

ROSE: Hi, honey. These old hats are becoming fashionable again. How do you like this one on me?

CHARLIE: I have to get myself together.

ROSE: (*Lightly, still trying on hats*) What's the matter?

CHARLIE: I had lunch with Michael. He called me up this morning after you went out and said he had to see me, that it was urgent. We met at the diner on 72nd street. That friend of his, Benton— what kind of a name is Benton?—told Michael he has to move out immediately.

ROSE: (*Lightly, still trying on hats*) But why all of a sudden?

CHARLIE: They were such wonderful friends. Everything was always great. (*Pause*) Now he doesn't want him in the house. . . . Because Michael has AIDS. . . . Michael is a homosexual.

ROSE: (*She stops dead in her tracks with a bright red hat on her head*) Our grandson has AIDS? He's a (*Can barely say the word*) homosexual? . . . It's not true!

CHARLIE: This afternoon he said, "Grandpa, I could never tell you this before." I used to joke with him. I would say, "Michaele, when are you getting married, a nice looking boy like you?" and he would say, "Grandpa, I'm waiting for someone like grandma, but I can't find her."

ROSE: (*She sits at table, DC*) I don't believe it.

CHARLIE: He told me himself.

ROSE: That lovely boy. That wonderful young man. It's just not possible.

CHARLIE: I'm disgusted with him. I've always been disgusted by homosexuals. I never could understand why they act that way. A few years ago I went into a movie house. I saw them. They did unnatural things to each other. Even animals don't do what they did.

146

ROSE: Calm down. I think there must be some mistake. It's just not like Michael. He had girlfriends. He even brought a girl here once. A very nice girl. Something has to be wrong.

CHARLIE: (*He takes her hand. Gently*) He's a homosexual. Homosexuals have girls as friends, but they like men more.

ROSE: What about this friend he's been living with?

CHARLIE: Michael said they were lovers.

ROSE: (*Pulls her hand away violently*) Oh, my god . . . I just can't accept it. This wonderful young man . . . This boy of ours. He was always so bright and handsome. He was normal all these years. How could he change all of a sudden?

CHARLIE: He didn't change. He was always a homosexual, but we didn't know it.

ROSE: Couldn't he see a psychiatrist? Maybe he could get help, and get himself straightened out.

CHARLIE: He told me he went for a while. But he couldn't change. He realized that was the way he was. He was only attracted to men.

ROSE: What do they do? What kind of a life is it? What is it to be a (*Pronounces it with distaste*) . . . homosexual?

CHARLIE: You don't know what a homosexual is?

ROSE: I know they live together. So. . . . what happens?

CHARLIE: They're lovers. As long as they're interested in each other, they stay together. For some of them it's like a marriage.

ROSE: (*Suddenly brightening*) Now that he's not going to be staying with Benton, maybe he can find someone else. Maybe he can find a girlfriend to live with.

CHARLIE: (*Trying to help her*) He has AIDS.

ROSE: (*Pause. She slumps*) Does that mean he's going to die?

CHARLIE: No, he says they have medication. He can live a long time.

ROSE: (*Beginning to catch on*) So . . . where is he going to live?

CHARLIE: That's why he wanted to see me. He's desperate. He spoke to Mary.

ROSE: (*Again brightening*) Oh, he can go back to live with his mother.

CHARLIE: No. Harry said, "I don't want him in the house." He's not Harry's son.

ROSE: But he's Mary's son. She has a right to have her son live with her.

CHARLIE: She can't fight Harry. A lot of people are afraid of AIDS. And he says he won't allow Michael to stay in the house.

ROSE: What would happen if he lives with them? You mean you can't use the same dishes, towels, and things like that? They're going to get AIDS from him?

CHARLIE: You don't get AIDS like that, Rose, darling. There's a lot of fear about it. It's like a plague. Harry forbade Mary to let Michael stay in the house.

ROSE: So . . . where is he going to go?

CHARLIE: That's why he had to speak with me. . . . He asked if we could take him in.

ROSE: We? (*Stands*) Charlie, I took care of your sick mother for years. I listened to all her complaints. I took care of her when she was so weak she couldn't get out of bed. When she died, God rest her soul, I thought, "Finally, I have a little freedom in my life" . . . . I can't handle a sick boy. I don't have the strength to take care of another sick person.

CHARLIE: Rose, he's our grandson. I would help you. . . .(*She isn't buying. He turns away*) When he said he was homosexual, I was so shocked I told him, "You disgust me."

ROSE: (*She turns and sits angrily*) That's a terrible thing to say to your grandson. As much as I dislike this whole business, I would never say that. How could you say that to your own grandson?

CHARLIE: I know . . . I feel terrible about it. He has no place to live. (*Pause*) I was thinking we could take him in temporarily.

ROSE: (*She has been staring into space*) Do you remember when he was about four years old and the photographer came to take pictures of the children at the nursery school? How he posed for the photographer? It was such an adorable picture.

CHARLIE: Oh, yes, the one on the dresser. He had all that curly hair and those big brown eyes. An angel face. I remember he'd say "Grandpa, sing 'A Capital Ship,'" and I would forget some of the words on purpose, and he would say, "No, no, Grandpa, it's 'the walloping window blind.'" And he was only two years old.

ROSE: How he learned to read all by himself.

CHARLIE: We were so proud of him. He was always winning prizes.

Remember he was the valedictorian in high school. And he made such a brilliant speech.

ROSE: He was so smart . . . I loved him so much . . .(*Pause*) . . . I still love him. . . . But I can't . . . I don't know what to do. Remember the time he came to the house and insisted on making dinner for us? He was so charming . . . I don't understand how he could have changed . . . become different.

CHARLIE: He didn't become different. We never know anybody completely. People tell us as much as they want to about themselves . . . But we don't know what they're really like. We thought we knew him but we didn't. (*Pause*) I used to wonder, "Why is he living with that Benton?" (*Pause. Then he grabs Rose's hands and bursts out*) I love him! He's not going to die. I won't let him go. I can't desert him. I have to stay close to him . . . Give him strength.

ROSE: (*She nods quietly*) I can't turn him away. I can't leave him with no place to go. I can't see him out on the street like a homeless person and no one to care for him. . . . (*Pause. Brightening*) I know. Why don't we invite him for dinner. I can make his favorite pot roast, and he loves my apple pie. (*Pause*) We'll find some way of taking care of him, one way or another . . . Okay, darling?

CHARLIE: Okay.

END

Time-Travel Scene
(From *It's About Time!*)[25]

This scene grew from a conversation in a workshop. Jen was about to grad-uate from college. Feeling a little panicky about being thrown out into the world of New York Theater, she had some escapist longings. She wondered if she might be happier as a stay-at-home wife and mother, like in the old days. All the older women said "no way!" But we wondered if they would have said that before Women's Liberation changed everything. So we set up some improvs in which Jen could go back in time, and this is one scene that grew out of them.

The characters are Jen (22), Muriel (an older woman playing herself in the present and then at twenty-two), the third character, Time, can be read in, because the real scene is between the two women. Props: you need a "baby" and a bottle; Costume: Jen should be very contemporary; Muriel changes quickly from contemporary to something that evokes a young mother in 1946. For the character of Time we used a top hat with a metronome painted on. Music: some science-fictiony time travel music will add to the playful mood of the scene.)

JEN: Muriel, I have a problem.

MURIEL: Well, you've come to the right place. Talk to the wise old woman. I'll set you on the right path.

JEN: Great! You see . . .

MURIEL: Wait, wise old women need to sit down to do their best thinking and advising.

She sits.

Now, tell.

JEN: Well, I'm just about to graduate from college and start my career. And I know I should focus on my career and I really want to. . . . But the fact is that right now all I can think about is want-ing to meet someone and settle down and just raise a good family.

MURIEL: Oi! Raising a family is wonderful, but wait until your career gets going. You've got at least twenty years to have children.

JEN: I know. That's what you say now, and I do too. But why do I have this other feeling so strongly! I wonder if we haven't all been brainwashed by Women's Liberation. I wonder what you would have said when you were my age, and you were a young mother. Were you dying to get out of the house and have a career then?

MURIEL: Well. . . .

JEN: I know, I want to go back to when you were twenty-two. I'm going to call time-out here. Time out!

TIME: Time in!

JEN: I want to go back in time.

TIME: Sorry, I don't do backwards. You'll have to ask Cousin Memory about that.

JEN: Please, I really need to know what it is just to be a mother and a wife.

TIME: Well, it might be amusing just this one time. Don't you just love how my name crops up everywhere? Choose your destination.

JEN: Muriel, what year were you twenty-two?

MURIEL: 1946. (*Time gestures her off stage as she goes off Right*) We were living in a small town in Maryland. In a Quonset hut. My husband had just come out of the army and . . .

JEN: Can I go now?

TIME: It's not that easy for you. I have to conjure you back in time—

Casting a spell.

> Tickity tockity
> Fum, fo fi fee
> Turn the clock back
> Endlessly
> Watch your swatch
> And big your Ben
> Then is now
> And now is then

Time-travel music comes up; Jen spins and flips through time. She lands next to Muriel, who has reappeared in 1940s costume, holding a baby.

MURIEL: (*Startled*) Who are you?

JEN: Hi, Muriel. Don't you recognize me? I'm Jen.

MURIEL: Well, you do look oddly familiar.

JEN: You don't remember?

MURIEL: No

JEN: You look great, so much . . . younger than . . . than . . . the last time I saw you.

MURIEL: Thanks. I just feel so much better since the war is over and my husband is working and the government gave us this Quonset hut to live in.

JEN: So this is a Quonset hut. It's really cute. I saw these in a documentary on TV.

MURIEL: TV? What's TV?

JEN: (*Looking for a TV*) Television?

MURIEL: Oh yeah, I saw that at the World's Fair in 1939. They said everyone could have one in their own home.

JEN: Everyone does . . . (*Gets it*) . . . where I come from.

MURIEL: Wow.

JEN: But the thing is it just becomes this big waste of time. People sit around watching Oprah all day long.

MURIEL: Opera?

JEN: No Oprah. This woman who has this talk show and people come on and tell about weird things they do like women who get tattoos all over their bodies or men who sleep with their baby sitters.

MURIEL: Yuck!

JEN: Yeah. . . . Your baby is so cute. What's her name?

MURIEL: Janice, she's just a year old. You want to feed her?

JEN: Can I? (*She takes baby and bottle*) I'm so glad to see you use cloth diapers.

MURIEL: What else is there?

JEN: I agree. It's so much more ecological.

MURIEL: Eco . . . what?

JEN: Ecological . . . ecology . . . like saving the environment from pollution.

MURIEL: What's pollution?

JEN: (*Sighs—to audience*) It really is a different world back here. . . . I would love to have a baby—they're so cute. . . . When did you stop breast feeding?

MURIEL: Oh, I never breast fed. My doctor was completely against it.

JEN: Why?

MURIEL: He said if I breast fed, I would gain a lot of weight, because you have to eat butter and cream to nourish the baby properly.

JEN: Are you kidding? No one thinks that any more . . . I mean where I come from.

MURIEL: Where *do* you come from?

JEN: Can you keep a secret?

MURIEL: Sure.

JEN: I come from the future.

MURIEL: Really? (*Jen nods*) Well, with all the things they say they can do with atomic energy these days, I guess anything is possible. What year do you come from?

JEN: 1996.

MURIEL: Wow, I would be . . . seventy years old! Will I still be alive then? . . . No no no, I don't want to know. . . . So, what's it like in 1996?

JEN: Well, it's really different. There's television, like I said and the telephones have push buttons instead of dials, and everyone has computers and . . .

MURIEL: Computers?

JEN: Oh, it's really hard to explain. And I don't want to ruin it for you, and I promised not to interfere. And anyway I don't think I have much time. So I want to ask you something. Are you happy being a housewife and a mother?

MURIEL: Of course I am. I love my baby and my husband has a good job at the hardware store. We do want a bigger apartment, though. This Quonset hut is so small. But it's only forty dollars a month.

JEN: Forty dollars a month? You know how much I pay? I share a two-bedroom apartment with this guy—strictly platonic—and we each pay $500 a month. And that's a bargain!

MURIEL: Oh God, I hope I don't live that long. I would wind up selling apples in the streets.

JEN: Don't worry, you'll be okay. . . . If you live that long. . . . But what I want to talk to you about is this one big change that's going to happen. In 1996, when I'm the same age as you are now, women have been liberated.

MURIEL: From what?

JEN: Well, from being housewives and mothers who depend on their husbands for their income and can't have careers of their own.

153

MURIEL: But why would they want to be liberated from that?

JEN: That's my question. You see, in 1996 women work just like men. Well, not just like, but we've made a lot of progress.

MURIEL: You mean like Rosie the riveter during the war?

JEN: Yes, she's one of our heroes. I want to be an actress and a dancer.

MURIEL: Wow! Someday I would love to act in a play.

JEN: Oh, you will. I mean, I really hope you will. So you're really happy being a housewife and a mother?

MURIEL: Sure!

JEN: Don't you want to work?

MURIEL: I work hard! You should try taking care of a baby and a house and a husband by yourself.

JEN: Oh I didn't mean that. I mean work, like a job.

MURIEL: Uh-uh! No, mam! I worked while my husband was in the army, and I'm glad I don't have to now. Maybe someday I'll get to travel and act in plays, but right now I'm happy enough, and when we get a washing machine and a better apartment and another baby in a year or so, I'll be even happier.

JEN: You know, you're much more optimistic than I am. We're the same age but I don't feel ready to get married. And I certainly can't bring a child into this world. I mean, I feel like a baby. How could I have a baby?

MURIEL: I feel like a baby too. But my mother helps me and I talk with my girlfriends, and there's this new book by Doctor Spock.

JEN: Spock? I thought he was killed off by the Klingons.

MURIEL: He was?

JEN: Yeah, in the first episode of *Star Trek The Next Generation*.

MURIEL: Oh, you're talking 1996 again.

JEN: Sorry. Oh, geez, speaking of Star Trek, I forgot to program my VCR. So I have to get back. Look, thanks for the visit. I'm sorry to run off. I gotta get back. (*Calls out*) Time! Are you there?

TIME: (*Has been sitting on UC bench watching or snoozing*) So where should I be, lassie?

JEN: Beam me back, Timey!

Time: Fee fie fo fum

First you go

154

And now you come!

JEN: You know you have really helped me a lot. Thanks, and . . . I'll see you . . . after a while. Goodbye.

The music starts again and Jen rocks and rolls through time. As she goes she yells back at Muriel.

By the way—you are going to be alive in 1996, and you will be fabulous!

MURIEL: (*Holding her baby*) What did she say?

END

Victor & Matt
(From *Three Sisters and a Brother*)[26]

This scene reverses the expectation that the younger man will seek advice from the older. Victor, a very successful businessman in his sixties has recently divorced after a long marriage and seeks the advice of twenty-something Matt about how to go about dating today.

VICTOR:: (*Uneasy, a little too friendly*) So tell me, Matt, you seem to have a nice girlfriend.

MATT: (*Guarded*) Yeah, Heather's great. (*Pause*)

VICTOR: So how does it go these days? . . . How do you ask a girl out? . . . What's a man supposed to do?

MATT: Well, first of all you don't say "girl"—you say woman. I was lucky with Heather. I met her in a bar. How did you meet your wife?

VICTOR: Actually it was arranged.

MATT: No!

VICTOR: We were betrothed in utero. Our mothers were pregnant at the same time.

MATT: You've got to be kidding!

VICTOR: It's God's honest truth.

MATT: Didn't you ever date?

VICTOR: No, nobody bothered me because they knew I was betrothed to her, and nobody bothered her because they knew she was betrothed to me.

MATT: How did you know if you liked each other?

VICTOR: Our parents liked each other. What else do you need?

MATT: How old were you when you got married?

VICTOR: Nineteen.

MATT: So then what did you do?

VICTOR: I joined her father's business, and we started having children.

MATT: I'm blown away! I don't know what I'd do if my parents had me "arranged." What if you ended up with some dud?

VICTOR: Well, we did get divorced after forty-five years, so it wasn't exactly a match made in heaven.

MATT: And now you want to ask someone out?

VICTOR: Right. Someone very special. (*They sit*)

MATT: So what are you going to do?

VICTOR: Well, I'm extremely busy next weekend, but I have managed to free up Saturday night, and I can squeeze her in at eight o'clock. I'll send the car around ahead of time, so she can't be late; I've reserved a table at the Pierre.

MATT: (*Acts impressed*) At the Pierre?

VICTOR: That's the best place, isn't it? I mean if you drop 300 dollars on a night out, a girl—

MATT: A woman.

VICTOR: A woman is going to have to know you're interested.

MATT: (*Shakes his head*) I dunno. It sounds to me like you're going about it the wrong way.

VICTOR: (*Surprised*) How so?

MATT: Let's start at the beginning. How do you even know your— Ms. X—is going to be free on Saturday night?

VICTOR: If she isn't, she'll make herself free.

MATT: Problem number 1: attitude. Number 2: how do you know Ms. X even likes the food at the Pierre?

VICTOR: (*Eagerly*) I've solved that one already. The best thing on the menu is the filet mignon. I'll order ahead of time. Filet mignon, petit pois, a green salad. *And*, their special Black Forest cake with fresh strawberries and whipped cream. No woman could object to that.

MATT: But, Victor, with all due respect, some women like to order dinner for themselves!

VICTOR: Next thing you'll be telling me they don't want me to pick up the check!

MATT: Well, some of them don't. They don't want to feel obligated.

VICTOR: But it *pleases* me to be generous!

MATT: I know, Victor. You're a very generous man. But it's how that generosity comes across. If you grab the check as soon as it arrives—well, that can be very offensive to a woman.

VICTOR: Offensive!

MATT: Overbearing.

VICTOR: Overbearing. (*Sighs*) So what you're telling me is *not* to send the car around; *not* to reserve my favorite table at the Pierre; and *not* to order ahead of time. I suppose next you're going to tell me not to buy flowers either. A nice corsage?

MATT: No, you can buy a corsage if you want to.

VICTOR: I can?

MATT: That's traditional.

VICTOR: But on the first date?

MATT: Believe me, that's okay. I bought irises for Heather the very first time we met, and tears came into her eyes.

VICTOR: (*Relieved*) Well, I'm glad some things haven't changed. I'll get the flowers. And afterwards, we'll take a hansom cab back through the park. That'll put her in the mood.

MATT: (*Wryly*) In the mood?

VICTOR: To invite me up. You know, when we get to her house. It's the least she can do after I've bought her dinner.

MATT: Hey, listen, slow down a moment.

VICTOR: It doesn't work like that any more?

MATT: Did it work like that in the past?

VICTOR: (*Shrugs*)

MATT: Scrap the hansom cab. Just *walk* her back through the park. And maybe she'll ask you up for a cup of coffee.

VICTOR: (*Suggestively*) I know about *that.*

MATT: Don't be too sure. Just because she asks you up, don't assume you're home free. The rules have changed. You could be sitting together on the sofa, and getting all cozy, and then suddenly she'll say, "Oh, I forgot to make the coffee!"

VICTOR: So I say, "Let's not bother about the coffee."

MATT: No, you *go and help her make it.* But remember, even if the kitchen is sort of small, and she bumps up against you as she reaches for the milk, that doesn't necessarily mean she's going to fall into your arms.

VICTOR: It doesn't?

MATT: It certainly does not. It may look like a yes, but in actual fact it is a no. And if she says, "Oh, my shoulders are stiff. Would you please give me a little back rub?"—

VICTOR: That's a yes?

MATT: No. That's still a no. Even if she looks at her watch and notices it's really getting late, and says how she'd hate to have you go home now—

VICTOR: *That's* a yes?

MATT: No. That's a no, too. And when she goes into the other room because she's finding her loose-fitting jeans just *so* constricting—

VICTOR: It's definite!

MATT: No, that's a no. I promise. That's a no too.

VICTOR: Oy!

MATT: See it's all gotten a lot more difficult.

VICTOR: You can say that again!

MATT: Look. I make the move. I could end up in *jail.* If I don't, she's beautiful and it's still worth it.

VICTOR: In other words, a man has to have a little moxy.

MATT: That's right! And it can work. Heather and I are doing great! And we've been together for six months!

END

Three-Person Scenes*

An Appalling Old Lady[27]
(From the play of the same name)

Sara is well into her eighties, in excellent health, and full of life. Her daughter Marge and son Mort are worried by the change in their mother. The poem is by Rumi, translation by Coleman Barks.[28]

Sara is reciting a poem. Marge is staring at her.

SARA: Just listen to this poem. (*Reads dramatically*)

There is some kiss we want
with our whole lives, the touch

of spirit on the body. Seawater
begs the pearl to break its shell.

And the lily, how passionately
It needs some wild darling!

At night, I open the window and ask
the moon to come and press its
face against mine.

Breathe into me. Close
the language door and open the love window.
The moon won't use the door,
only the window.

MARGE: Mother, are you sure you're all right? You don't look so good. Not your usual self.
SARA: I was joyously happy this morning. The beautiful snowfall filled me with ecstasy and then—
MARGE: Mother, be serious. I'm concerned about you.
SARA: Concerned?
MARGE: Yes, I just wanted to drop by to check up on you. See if you needed anything.

---

*See pages 17, 43, 53, 82, and 122 for other three- or more person scenes.

160

SARA: I'm fine. Totally self-sufficient. Do you want something?

MARGE: No. I get by. Of course I work all week. Then I come home, prepare dinner and wash the dishes. And do all the other chores because the children never help me.

SARA: I see Sue sometimes. But how are Jenny and . . .

MARGE: Sabrina.

SARA: Yes, Sabrina. My lovely grandchildren. How are they doing these days?

MARGE: They're fine. Except for the fighting. Whining, complaining, cursing. No father to keep them in line.

SARA: You're lucky you're the one in charge.

MARGE: I only have four small rooms so we're always on top of each other. (*Bell rings and then rings again*) Mother, the doorbell.

SARA: I didn't hear it.

Bell rings again.

MARGE: You don't hear a lot of things. (*Pause*) I'll get it.

MORT: Oh, you're here. When I rang and rang and nobody answered I started to get worried.

MARGE: Look at her. She's acting funny. Maybe you can talk sense to her.

MORT: I came to see our darling mother who never answers the phone.

MARGE: She's losing her mind. Ranting and raving poetry. (*Quotes*) "the moon won't use the door," or something. Never heard anything like it.

SARA: (*Quotes pointedly*)
"Close the language door,
And open the love window."

MORT: Ma, you look different. Are you all right? Recognize me? (*She makes dismissive gesture*)

MORT: (*Pause.*) I think this place is wearing you out. It's so huge. Three bedrooms—seven rooms. Taking care of it must be an ordeal.

MARGE: There's dust everywhere. You'll get buried here without even knowing it.

SARA: To hell with the dust. I enjoy looking at my books—you know I have a passion for poetry.

MORT: And what else? You're never home.

MARGE: Like mother, like son.

SARA: I like to go out.

MARGE: Go out?

MORT: Where?

SARA: To the comedy clubs. I spend time with the young people.

MARGE: How could you? You never went out when father was alive.

MORT: At your age, you could overdo it. And then where would you be?

SARA: At home with my friends.

MARGE: Your friends? Strangers from the club come here?

MORT: You're risking your life. You could get robbed, stabbed, or even worse.

SARA: Lots of people come here. I radiate charm. People flock to me.

MARGE: The guy we passed in the hall who said hello. Who is he?

SARA: An architect, Michael. We have tea regularly.

MARGE: I think he's a (*Whispers*) homosexual.

SARA: So what if he is?

MARGE: You could get AIDS using the same cup or plate.

SARA: Nonsense.

MARGE: You have to be careful, mother. You're not taking precautions.

SARA: (*Coyly*) Oh yes, I am.

MORT: (*Trying to charm her*) This place is really too big for you. You're wearing yourself out. You're getting so thin. I can hardly see you.

SARA: Maybe I just move too fast for you.

MARGE: The children and I could really use those extra rooms.

MORT: I could use the space for photographic shoots. Such stylish surroundings.

MARGE: All you want to do is bring nude models, your so-called dates, here to impress them. I know you.

SARA: But I need space for my friend Claudio. I'm enjoying myself for the first time in years.

MARGE: Father would turn over in his grave.

MORT: Mother, at your age.

SARA: Yes, at my age. I like to wake up in the morning with someone next to me. Don't you?

MARGE: You're acting like a teenager.

SARA: It's so romantic.

Marge and Mort rise and talk over Sara as if she isn't there or can't hear. Sara follows them as if she were watching a ping-pong match.

MARGE: This can't go on. Orgies every night.

MORT: She'll get ripped off.

MARGE: She'll end up in the hospital.

MORT: Or worse.

MARGE: She picks up these men in comedy clubs.

MORT: They're only after one thing—her money.

MARGE: She's too trusting.

MORT: Naive.

MARGE: Gullible.

MORT: She can't live alone anymore. (*They move in on her*)

MARGE: Mother, we found a lovely place in Croton-on-Hudson, where you'd be so happy. They have lovely grounds.

MORT: Refined people. Dignified people. Your own age. With your interests.

MARGE: Luxurious rooms and gourmet food.

MORT: And I hear the view of the river is breathtaking at any hour.

MARGE: They even have lectures and poetry readings.

SARA: It sounds wonderful—

MARGE: I'm glad you think so because we—

SARA: For you.

MARGE: For me?

SARA: I'm rooted in this place. I derive nourishment from these surroundings.

MARGE: Mother, you never take my advice.

MORT: Ma, we're only thinking of your own good.

SARA: I'm not going anywhere. I wish to come and go as I please. And the last breath I'll take, whenever that is, will be in my own house, in my own bed with whomever I want to be with. (*She starts to exit*) I'm expecting company and I never keep my friends waiting, but you're welcome to stay while I change.

Marge and Mort watch her leave, then look at each other, out at audience, and then shrug together.

END

3 Girls
(from *Béçoming Åmèriçañ*)[29]

The play was to be about immigration, but we learned quickly that most of the Roots and some Branches shared the experience of being children of immigrants. So the play became more about assimilation. One aspect of being a child of immigrants is the sense that you have to learn about America for yourself, that your parents can't help much. This scene came from an improv that included both Roots and Branches, but it can be played by actors of any age. The three girls are sitting on a stoop on the Lower East Side in the middle of the Depression. But we have found that the time, languages referred to, and cultural references can be transposed to any time.

MARCY: I'm so upset. I just found out my mother isn't a real American. She was born in America, but she still isn't a real American.

MURIEL: Why not?

MARCY: She didn't grow up here. She was born here but then Grandma and Grandpa took her back to Poland when she was only six months old. I used to be so proud of how she would come to school, so tall and beautiful in her purple dress and high heels, and I thought she was the best and so American! And lots of my friends had parents who weren't born in America, and my mom was, and that's a big deal. But today she said, "Don't bother me I'm tinkink." And I said "Mom, how come you talk with that accent if you were born in America?" And she told me yeah she was born here, but they took her back to Poland when she was six months old! I'm so upset.

MURIEL: Well, my mother was born here and she didn't go back when she was six months old. But you think you have problems! My father was born in Poland. And he has this very weird way of talking. This terrible accent. All words that start with "v" he pronounces as "w." "Vat are you bringing me vater ven I vant wodka?!" And I want to tell him, "Dad that's not the right way to say it," but if I ever said that to him, he might smack me. I'm just so embarrassed in front of my friends. I know he tries so hard to be an American, but I mean he wears plaid pants with multicolored jackets.

SARA: Isn't that so embarrassing? You don't want to be seen in public with that.

MURIEL: Exactly.

SARA: It's awful.

MARCY: Oh, my Dad's smell. He smells like Lucky Strikes and saw-dust and he talks kind of almost continental.

MURIEL: Really? Where was he born?

MARCY: Poland. But I think it was like near Germany, Poland.

MURIEL: You think that makes a difference?

SARA: Near Germany, Poland?

MARCY: Well, I don't know. He speaks kind of German, kind of Jewish. "Continental."

MURIEL: "Continental?" Does he use a cigarette holder when he smokes?

MARCY: No, but my mother does. She's an actress!

MURIEL: Are you lying?

SARA: She's lying.

MARCY: She is an actress. She really is.

MURIEL: Did she ever play in a movie?

MARCY: Well, no.

MURIEL: So what did she play in?

MARCY: You know, the stage.

MURIEL: The stage. I've never seen anything on the stage.

MARCY: You've never been to the theater?

MURIEL: No.

MARCY: Oh, it's so wonderful.

MURIEL: Is it expensive?

MARCY: A little bit expensive. But they have it so you can stand in the back.

MURIEL: And what is it like?

MARCY: Well, they don't speak English . . .

SARA: Oh, so it's one of those Yiddish theaters.

MARCY: Yeah, so?

SARA: It's not a real theater.

MARCY: I don't think so! I don't think so! It's just the same. They stand on a stage and they do things and they say things.

MURIEL: Yeah, but would you want to take your friends there? I mean, you can't understand anything because

SARA: . . . They don't speak English!

MURIEL: In case you hadn't noticed, this is America.

MARCY: You don't know what you're talking about!

MURIEL: I do so, I'm going to be fifteen on my next birthday.

MARCY: Well, I'm going to be fifteen on my next to next birthday.

MURIEL: So, you're much younger than I am.

MARCY: That doesn't mean you know everything.

MURIEL: Oh, I know plenty. I know almost everything there is to know. My parents think I know nothing, but I really know more than they do.

SARA: (*Seizing an opportunity*) Have you had that curse yet?

MURIEL: What do you mean? You mean the bloody thing? My mother said that's no curse, that's just being a woman. Yes, I've had it since I'm twelve and a half. And what's more I'm proud of it.

SARA: Proud of it?

MURIEL: Sure.

MARCY: But, it's like every month you bleed, right?

MURIEL: Yeah, it's disgusting, but it means that you're a real woman, and you can have babies very quickly, VERY QUICKLY. And if you don't want babies you have to sit on the side of the chair. (*They all do*) No, you got to sit like this. (*They all shift*) You got to sit right on the edge.

SARA: Did your mother teach you this?

MURIEL: No, no—my girlfriend Nellie. She's going to be seventeen. She knows things.

SARA: Where is she from?

MURIEL: Oh, she was born here. She's got big breasts—whew! She thinks she's pregnant a lot of the time so she sits like this a lot.

MARCY: I wouldn't sit like that. I wouldn't want anyone to know I was pregnant. They'd have to send you away.

MURIEL: Why?

MARCY: They don't want you home. I saw it in the movies.

SARA: They want to hide the baby. My mother told me about her sister in Russia. She had to be sent away.

MURIEL: Because she didn't sit on the edge of the chair that's why. In case you are—then the whole thing goes away. In case you're a little bit pregnant.

SARA: How can you be a little bit pregnant?

MURIEL: That's what Nellie told me. She told me if you think you're a little pregnant you have to sit right over here—right here.

SARA: And you believe everything you hear?

MURIEL: From Nellie, yes.

SARA: My grandmother's been around too. I don't see you taking advice from my grandmother.

MURIEL: What does your grandmother know?

SARA: She knows a lot. A lot more than Nellie.

MURIEL: Where was she born? Where was your grandmother born?

SARA: In the old country.

MURIEL: So an old country, old lady knows a lot. Come on!

SARA: So is that it, we're just deciding that people who were born here are smarter?

MURIEL: Yeah.

SARA: Well, I don't know. My mother wasn't born here and she's still smart. She speaks Jewish and she speaks Russian, and she speaks a little German . . .

MURIEL: So what, this is America. Can your mother speak American?

SARA: I used to try to teach her how to say certain words . . .

MURIEL: But, they never lose that stupid accent, right? They go through their whole lives with those stupid accents and they never learn. Never.

SARA: I taught my Mom how to swear in English. She doesn't know any other words. Nellie sure knows how to swear in English though; I've heard her talk. She's a bad influence on you.

MURIEL: She is not. This girl knows everything—everything.

SARA: Everything about nothing.

MURIEL: Everything about life. You know—this thing called life.

MARCY: She does things with boys.

MURIEL: So what?

SARA: You don't do that do you?

MURIEL: Not very often.

MARCY: You have to be a virgin.

MURIEL: I'm a virgin.

SARA: But your friend isn't.

MURIEL: Yes she is!

SARA: I don't think so.

MARCY: A lot of people pretend to be, but aren't. I saw that in the movies. And my sister's boyfriend told me that the lions in front of the 42nd Street Library on 5th Avenue, they made them so they'd roar whenever a virgin walks by. Well, I sat there for a whole afternoon watching girls walk up and down the steps and they never roared once!

MURIEL: That's stupid. They're statues! I know Nellie's a virgin.

MARCY: How many times have you seen her sitting on the edge of her chair?

MURIEL: She's just that kind of girl, she gets around a lot. But I like her. I really do. She lets me do things with her.

SARA: What kind of things?

MURIEL: Can't tell. We crossed fingers.

MARCY: Like play spin the bottle at parties?

MURIEL: Once in a while.

SARA: What's that?

MURIEL: If you win, you get to "French kiss" with a boy.

(*The others gasp*)

SARA: Is that like kissing on the hand?

MURIEL: Don't be silly. With all the languages spoken in your house, you don't know what French kissing is?

SARA: Very funny, Muriel.

MURIEL: I can't believe it.

MARCY: Even I know.

SARA: Tell me.

MURIEL: It's when you go in the corner with a boy and he sticks it in your mouth.

SARA: What?

MURIEL: The tongue.

SARA: Aggggh! That is disgusting.

MURIEL: Only because you haven't done it.

SARA: If some guy ever kissed me and put his tongue in my mouth . . .

MURIEL: You'll like it.

MARCY: I gotta go.

MURIEL: Just when it's getting good, she's gotta go!

END

Appendix 2

A Complete Listing of Roots&Branches Plays

Interested groups and individuals should contact the company. All plays directed and co-authored by Arthur Strimling.

I Am Acting My Age (1991), Howard Pflanzer, co-author. An exploration of stereotypes about age, ageism, and aging. We quickly discover that segregation of the generations in our culture makes elders as prone to stereotypical thinking as the young. Working together cut through the stereotypes—we became individuals to each other, with individual strengths, weaknesses, styles, and ages. Then it became fun to play within the preconceptions. This is a useful place to begin any intergenerational process.

Romeo & Juliet and Juliet & Romeo and Romeo & Juliet (1992) Christian McEwen, co-author. Shakespeare is the frame for an examination of romantic love within and between generations. Three pairs of star-crossed lovers meet on a romantic Shakespearean cruise on the SS *Verona*. The first couple are both in their 70s; in the second, the male is in his 60s, the female in her early 20s; the third, the male is 22, the female is 86. They all fall in love and work out their own, very different, destinies.

Three Sisters and a Brother (1993), Christian McEwen, co-author. Three elderly sisters, Olga, Marsha, and Irene, and their bookish unsuccessful brother, Andrew, gather with their children and grandchildren at the family country home, to celebrate Irene's 90th birthday. The house is filled with the past. A hilarious dinner scene is spoiled when Olga berates Andrew for having forced her to sacrifice her life for the family. Andrew was the only one the family could afford to send to college, but he did nothing with his education except read books. The evening ends in dreams of past and future.

Old AIDS (1994), Christian McEwen, co-author. Two grandparents learn that their beloved grandson is gay, has AIDS, and wants to come and live with them. The only play we know of that deals with AIDS from the perspective of the elderly.

An Appalling Old Lady (1994), Howard Pflanzer, co-author. At 90, Sarah is changing her ways: she reads and writes poetry, goes to comedy clubs with her granddaughter, dresses flamboyantly. She even takes a lover. Her middle-aged son and daughter are alarmed. They plot to talk her into moving into a home. But their motives are not entirely altruistic: each sees the opportunity to get Sarah's spectacular rent-controlled river-view apartment. The confrontation scene is a perennial hit with our audiences. Based on a short story by Bertolt Brecht.

Lookin' Good! A Follies (1995), David Schechter, co-author. About looks and beauty, a wonderfully loaded topic when the age range goes from 19 to 90. Constructed like an old-fashioned follies, the show features a "Beauty Pageant Through the Ages" and variety acts including "The Make-up Follies;" "The Exercise Follies;" "Dr. Nipntuck, the Magic Plastic Surgeon;" "The Incredible Vanishing Woman ('Look! As she ages, she disappears!')"; and "The Wisdom Strip."

It's About Time! (1996), David Schechter, co-author. Looks at Time, as its meanings change across the life course. Time is an actual character, holding everyone hostage until the gun goes off for "The Human Race." Later, a 22-year-old, torn between career and motherhood, travels back in time to meet one of the elderly characters in the late 1940s, when she was a 22-year-old housewife and mother. The climax is a searing monologue/song, in which a woman relates her twenty-year battle with cancer and how it has affected her relationship with time.

Béçoming Åmèriçañ (1997), David Schechter, co-author. About immigration and assimilation. Scenes range from hilarious to poignant—an intense argument over the basic issue of whether Chinese food is Jewish or American; an eight-year-old, tormented by older kids wants to hide her identity and become a "real American;" three teenagers in the 1930s decide that because their parents don't know English, they don't know anything, and get into some strange ideas about how sex works. At the end the Statue of Liberty is cloned and all the clones argue about immigration policy past and present.

Revival of the Fittest (1998). Best scenes and short plays from the previous years.

The Subway Series (2000), David Schechter, co-author. A subway car magically travels through time as well as space. At the start of the ride, young and old passengers are pitted against each other. Then we travel back to look at life in several decades, coming to rest in 1942, when most of the elders were about the age of the students. Scenes of marriage and work reveal how different styles, language, even love itself were back then—the popular WWII hit, "Don't Sit Under The Apple Tree (With Anyone Else but Me)" is background to a romantic scene in 1942, and then rewritten as it might be sung today: *Don't go getting down on your knee/ Till I finish my MD/ Make partner or VP/ Or possibly all three/No no no/ I'm not getting myself tied down/To those hormones and chemistry/I'd rather live alone*. The climactic scene, built around one of the young people's true story of the extraordinary risks she took in support of abortion rights, brings old and young together in hope and struggle from generation to generation.

Playing Lear (2001–2002), with David Schechter. A rehearsal of *King Lear* is constantly interrupted and disrupted as the actors interject scenes, stories, and opinions from their own lives that reflect the great struggles in the play. Jealousy, flattery, parental tyranny, the ingratitude of children, generational struggles for freedom and security. Finally the great reconciliation scene between Lear and Cordelia provokes beginnings of reconciliation between the actors and generational demons that haunt them. This much praised production was featured at the International Festival of Senior Theatre in 2002 and invited to be performed at the United Nations Plenary Session on September 12, 2001.

Growing Up/Growing Down (2003), David Schechter, author/director, with Arthur Strimling. Original songs by David Schechter. Fairy tales are the springboard for this fantasy examination of the power of iconic figures like the beautiful princess, the handsome prince, the wicked stepmother, the witch, hag, or crone, the frog, the wolf, and other animals. Telling their own lives as fairy tales, the beautiful princess escapes from the three bedroom cage/castle and her no-longer-so-handsome prince and runs off to Single Woods, where, she "kissed a lot of princes that turned into frogs," before she finds the frog that becomes her true partner. And the bad rap that old women get in fairy tales—"hag, witch, and so on"—is transformed through song into a recipe for how to become a Juicy Crone.

Notes

1. *Playing Lear* by Arthur Strimling with David Schechter and the Ensemble (Roots&Branches 2002).
2. Robert N. Butler, "The Life Review: An Interpretation of Reminiscence in the Aged" in *Middle Age and Aging*, edited by Berinice L. Neugarten (Chicago University Press, 1968). *Number Our Days* by Barbara Myerhoff (Simon & Schuster, 1978) is, among other things, the classic introduction to the meaning of reminiscence in the elderly, and certainly the most readable. If you read only one book about aging, this is the one.
3. Anne Davis Basting, unpublished memo. See also her important book, *The Stages of Age* (Michigan, 1998), which deals in-depth with a wide variety of senior theater groups.
4. Lyrics and music by David Schechter (2003).
5. *Growing Up/Growing Down* by David Schechter with Arthur Strimling and the Ensemble (Roots&Branches 2003). Lyrics and music by David Schechter. Michael Rubinowitz contributed to the Juicy Crone recipe.
6. Dr. Johnetta B. Cole, now President of Bennett College, said this in a speech at the Hunter School of Social Work in about 1985.
7. Phone interview with Yvette Pollack.
8. *I Am Acting My Age* by Arthur Strimling, Howard Pflanzer and the Ensemble (Roots&Branches 1991).
9. *Playing Lear* by Arthur Strimling with David Schechter and the Ensemble. "Song of Flattery" by David Schechter (Roots& Branches 2002).
10. The idea for this comes from Barbara Myerhoff, who, in *Number Our Days*, vividly describes her relationship with the old tailor Shmuel.
11. Harlow put baby monkeys in cages, some with a puppet mother

made solely of wire, and some with mothers made of wire covered with terry cloth. The babies with terry cloth mothers cuddled up to them and thrived, while the babies with wire mothers became severely depressed, stopped eating, and died. Even when offered the choice between wire mothers that gave milk and terry cloth mothers that did not, the babies chose the terry cloth mothers.

Ida, one of the original seniors in Roots&Branches, made it her weekly practice to hug every person in the group as they came in.

12. Andy Greenhouse in a conversation after a show.
13. *The Subway Series* by Arthur Strimling with David Schechter and the Ensemble. Lyrics by David Schechter and Arthur Strimling (Roots&Branches 2000).
14. I heard Barbara say this many times in our workshops. I don't know if she ever wrote it.
15. *Three Sisters and a Brother* by Arthur Strimling and Christian McEwen with the Ensemble (Roots&Branches 1992).
16. Robert Coles, *The Old Ones of New Mexico* (University of New Mexico Press 1973).
17. *Lookin' Good! A Follies* by Arthur Strimling, David Schechter, and the Ensemble (Roots&Branches 1995).
18. *Playing Lear* by Arthur Strimling with David Schechter and the Ensemble (Roots&Branches 2002).
19. I am no scholar of Shakespeare, but I have closely looked at the Variorum and many other editions of *King Lear*, interpretive essays, and asked a number of Shakespeare experts.
20. Peter Pitzele in private correspondence.
21. Helen M. Luke, *Old Age: Journey Into Simplicity* (Parabola Press, 1988).
22. *It's About Time!* by Arthur Strimling, David Schechter, and the Ensemble (Roots&Branches 1996).
23. *Romeo & Juliet and Juliet & Romeo and Romeo & Juliet*, by Arthur Strimling, Christian McEwen, Howard Pflanzer, and the Ensemble (Roots and Branches 1992).
24. *I Am Acting My Age*, by Arthur Strimling, Howard Pflanzer, and the Ensemble (Roots&Branches 1991).

25. *It's About Time!*, by Arthur Strimling, David Schechter, and the Ensemble (Roots&Branches 1996).
26. *Three Sisters and a Brother*, by Arthur Strimling and Christian McEwen with the Ensemble (Roots&Branches 1992).
27. *An Appalling Old Lady*, by Arthur Strimling, Howard Pflanzer, and the Ensemble (Roots&Branches 1994).
28. Coleman Barks, *Rumi: The Book of Love* (Harper, 2003), pp. 33–34.
29. *Béçoming Åmèriçañ*, by Arthur Strimling, with David Schechter, and the Ensemble (Roots&Branches 1997).